Living The Liturgy

A practical guide for participating in the
Divine Liturgy of the
Eastern Orthodox Church

by Stanley Samuel Harakas

F Z̥O S̥
E

Published with the approval of the Presbyters'
Council of the Greek Orthodox Archdiocese
through its Publications Committee.

LIGHT & LIFE PUBL. CO.

1974

"To him who loves us and has freed us from our sins by his blood and made us a kingdom, priests to his God and Father, to him be glory and dominion for ever and ever. Amen" (Revelation: 1:5-6)

and

To my Father who has given me a lifelong example of Christian living both inside and outside the temple of the Lord.

Prologue

"Living the Liturgy," is the account of a personal experience and enjoyment of the author. I hope and as a matter of fact I expect it to be both a challenge and a guide for the reader. A challenge because very few of us do live the exalting spiritual beauty and experience of the Divine Liturgy; a guide for we all need to be guided through the dramatic sequences of the liturgical text and celebration and be helped in our effort to ascend unto higher and loftier levels of inspiration and theosis.

It is in this spirit that we recommend wholeheartedly this book to the Clergy and the *pleroma* of our Holy Church for we believe that it can be of great value and usefulness to all.

Archbishop Iakovos

Table of Contents

A Necessary Introduction

"I Don't Get Anything Out of Going to Church"

Many years ago I wrote a very short article with a rather long title: "I Don't Get Anything Out of Going to Church." The article has been reprinted many times in parish bulletins, periodicals, youth magazines and even in an Armed Services Chaplain's magazine. The appeal of this short article was that it pointed (through its title) to a very common and widely felt complaint among Orthodox Christian laymen and laywomen. For many of the Orthodox faithful the Divine Liturgy is a rich and meaningful experience. For numerous others, however, the Liturgy is a closed book. A vast number of Orthodox Christians attend because it is "proper" to do so; because their religious feelings, in some vague and undefined way, are "satisfied"; because they feel that in order to be Christian they must be present at worship. But multitudes attend the Divine Liturgy on any given Sunday and feel no gain for it. Again and again, young and old, men and women, teenagers and even children, in their most honest moments, express an inward dissatisfaction and sense of frustration with attendance at the Divine Liturgy. The title of that article seemed to express that popularly felt response. Sincere Orthodox Christians, willing and eager to find the worship of their Church meaningful and inspiring, were disappointed.

The article itself shifted the responsibility for this deplorable situation from the Liturgy itself, or the language of the Service, or its length, or the Priest's voice, to the Christian worshipper himself! The concluding paragraphs of the article pointed to the need for active participation in the Divine Liturgy on the part of the Orthodox Christian worshipper. In part the article said:

> Very few things come to us without some effort. The greatest of experiences in our lives are never without cost.

You must work very hard to obtain an education; you must expend great effort to be a success in business, or the arts, or even at your daily job. Should we be surprised that the same holds true for our Worship experience? You must give in order to receive.

If you really expect to "get something" out of Church attendance, you must give. It is not enough just to sit in Church. You must take an active part in its worship. You must learn to participate personally and individually in the Service. This takes some effort. You first must learn what is being done in the Church Service.

Many excellent, yet inexpensive books can give you all you need of this information, if you are not able to obtain it from your Pastor.

The need for active participation is at the heart of this book. It is the key to successful and meaningful attendance at the Divine Liturgy. Thus, that article is the beginning of this book, providing it with its basic and essential idea. But, it is also the beginning of this book in a very different way. The "excellent and inexpensive books" do exist, but they all fix their attention primarily on the Service itself. They do not emphasize in detail and with clarity the manner and mode of *participation* on the part of the worshipper. That is what this book seeks to do. It is written in order to help you to participate positively and meaningfully in the Divine Liturgy in a moving and satisfying way. Experience has shown that *if you are interested, and if you follow the principles and methods outlined in this book, the Liturgy in all likelihood will rapidly become a richly meaningful and inspiring experience for you Sunday after Sunday.*

However, this book, makes some assumptions about you, the reader. First, it assumes that you are a member of the Orthodox Church, or are very much interested in its liturgical life; it assumes that you hold to the Christian Faith and have a measure of love for and loyalty to the Orthodox Church.

Secondly, it assumes that you are one of the many Orthodox Christians or interested persons who do not fully understand what occurs during the Divine Liturgy and that you "don't get very much out of going to Church."

7

This book, thirdly, takes for granted that you have an uneasy and unhappy feeling about this state of affairs and that you would like to do something about it in order to correct it. There is no amount of formal knowledge or theological training which can give you this interest and concern. Without it, this book can do little for you. Personal interest and the willingness to expend some effort are absolute necessities for success.

Finally, the book assumes that you will read through to the end and put these principles into action. When you do, you can expect to discover the many spiritual and moral, human and divine, religious and worldly experiences which the Divine Liturgy can give. You will experience the power of the Holy Spirit grow in your life and you will see a new awareness for the Church grow in you. The Church will cease to be a building and will become, as you grow into the spirit of the Divine Liturgy, a people, a worshipping community, the body of Christ! If you make a sincere effort on the basis of the ideas and methods presented here, the Divine Liturgy will be a more meaningful and vital experience for you.

Three Keys Which Open the Door to the Liturgy

In order to help you discover the riches of the Divine Liturgy, so that it might be a living firsthand experience for you, there are three keys which require your comprehension and understanding. None of these keys, as we present them in this book is beyond the comprehension of the average Orthodox Christian. In fact, they are so simple it is strange that they have been overlooked in the past.

The first key to a meaningful participation in the Divine Liturgy is a basic Liturgical and Sacramental understanding. It is necessary for you to know what the Divine Liturgy is, why the worship of the Church on Sunday mornings is sacramental, what the sacramental nature of Orthodox Christian worship means for our practical, day to day lives as Christians and members of the Orthodox Church. These truths are essentials. You cannot really worship "in spirit and in truth" as Jesus requires if these things are not clear. In other words, you must be able to put the Liturgy in a larger perspective if you are going to enter into its spirit and participate in it fully.

This, however, does not mean that you need a theological education to do so. The few, basic and elementary, Christian presuppositions which you must have are given in the first chapter of this book. You certainly are encouraged to read more about the faith and practice of our Church, especially its liturgical life. More and more is being written and published in English on these topics, and you would do well to inform yourself. But for now, what you need to know for meaningful participation in the Divine Liturgy is included in chapter one, entitled "Liturgical Living."

The second key which you must have is the knowledge of the basic structure of the present day form of the Divine Liturgy. As we look at the Divine Liturgy in its entirety as it is conducted in the Orthodox Church *today* in our parishes, we can discover a basic structure or pattern in it. If you see this pattern, you can adapt yourself and your participation to it. *This pattern applies only to the present form of the Liturgy.* In the long history of the development of the Liturgy, other patterns and other forms of structure existed. We do not ignore them, but the structure to which we point our readers is based on the present make-up and pattern of the Divine Liturgy. The structure provides the points of reference for the average Orthodox Christian to participate actively in the Divine Liturgy. This basic structure of the present-day form of the Liturgy is the second necessary key to the method presented in this book and it is described in Chapter Two, "The Living Liturgy."

The third key is the practical and realistic definition of what it means to participate in the Divine Liturgy. How do you, the worshipper, enter into the liturgical practice of Sunday morning worship? What are the specific ways in which you can actually participate in the Divine Liturgy? Perhaps this is the most useful part of the book. Avoiding both vague generalities and rigid prescriptions, you will learn in chapter three, through precept and example, the concrete ways by which the Orthodox Christian can actively relate to the various elements of the Liturgy. The practical ways of participating in the Divine Liturgy are, then, the third key with which we open the door to the richly rewarding experience that the Divine Liturgy can be for you. You will read about them in Chapter Three, "Live the Liturgy."

These three keys open the door to our participation in the Divine Liturgy. They permit us to pass through the door and enter the Liturgy itself. We will do that in the following two chapters which bear the same title: "Life in the Liturgy." In these chapters we go through the Divine Liturgy together, word for word and phrase by phrase, indicating its significance for you, showing you how to consciously and spiritually enter into each of the parts of the Divine Liturgy. Each section of the Divine Liturgy forms a subsection of these Chapters. Properly, they would form one chapter only. But because of the length, the one long chapter is divided into two smaller ones.

The final chapter, "The Liturgy Alive" is a handbook of the Divine Liturgy with participation instructions for your use as you attend the Liturgy, if you so choose. However, the principles outlined here can be put into practice with the aid of any other Liturgy-book which you might have at hand. If, for instance, your parish or jurisdiction has an official "Liturgical Book" in the pews of your parish Church, these principles can be readily put into practice with that specific book in your hands. For that matter, experience has shown that many people soon dispense with the use of the book completely once they have learned to put these methods into practice. What you bring to the Liturgy in the way of faith, understanding and the readiness to participate is much more significant than the book you hold in your hands.

An Invitation to You

Thus, I extend an invitation to you to read this book carefully and thoughtfully. When you have read it and when you have absorbed its ideas, take those ideas to

Church with you. Put them into practice! Participate actively in the Divine Liturgy! The Service will in all likelihood become more interesting, meaningful, and significant. You will begin to grow in the spiritual life and you will experience new implications of Church membership and Christian brotherhood. Your active daily life will take on new and inspiring dimensions and you will find that life itself will become more full and abundant!

Here, then, is an invitation to discover for yourself the new and enriching experience of liturgical participation. You are invited to enter into the reality of not merely "following" or "attending" or "going to" the Divine Liturgy but of truly and fully "Living the Liturgy"!

Much gratitude is due to many people for many kindnesses and much assistance leading to the publication of this little book. First, I must thank the many people who listened to the ideas before they were ever committed to paper. They lived them, questioned them, practiced them, evaluated them and enriched them by their own contributions. Over one hundred converts, many numbers of lecture and class audiences and not a few congregations have helped develop the thoughts and practices presented here.

I am very grateful to my own Archbishop, the Primate of the Greek Orthodox Church of North and South America and Patriarchal Exarch in the Americas, His Eminence Archbishop Iakovos, not only for his sensitive preface, but also for asking the Presbyters' Council of the Archdiocese to review the book before publication.

To the members of the Publications Committee of the Presbyter's Council I am deeply and specifically indebted. All six members of the committee read the manuscript and provided invaluable criticisms, most of which led to revisions and changes in either format or content. These beloved brethren in the Lord's service are the Rev. Alkiviadis C. Calivas, the Rev. Anthony Coniaris, the Rev. Evagoras Constantinides, the Rev. Anthony Gergiannakis, the Rev. Constantine M. Monios and the Rev. Nicholas C. Triantafilou.

In addition, I must express from this place my sincere

appreciation to all the members of the Presbyters' Council for their unprecedented endorsement of the book at their September 24 and 25, 1973 meeting in New York City. I trust that their decision to endorse the contents of this book will encourage many of my fellow priests in Orthodox Churches where English is read to use it to help make the Divine Liturgy a more living experience for all the faithful Orthodox Christians in their charge.

I am also indebted to several other readers of the manuscript whose evaluations have proven most useful: The Rev. Dr. Nicon Patrinacos, Director of Publications of the Greek Orthodox Archdiocese, my former professor and Dean; Dr. George Bebis, my colleague on the Faculty of Holy Cross Greek Orthodox School of Theology who read the manuscript for accuracy as to the liturgical facts as presented here; the Rev. Anthony Coniaris, pastor and author, whose suggestions, guidance and encouragement were invaluable; Dr. Albert Stone, Professor of English at Hellenic College, Brookline, Mass., who read the manuscript with the critical eye of an expert in the clear use of the English language. All these friends have given generously of their time and judgment. I have pondered carefully all that has been suggested by the many readers of the manuscript and I have incorporated what I felt to be helpful for the reader. For the underlying concepts of this method of participation in the Divine Liturgy and for the errors of fact, form and judgment, I alone must be held responsible.

Finally, the "flesh of my flesh, and bone of my bones," my wife, Emily, must be acknowledged here. She has not only provided me with inspiration, encouragement and loving support, but she has also typed the manuscript several times over, during the process of its preparation for the press. No words can express my debt to her.

Holy Cross Greek Orthodox
School of Theology
Brookline, Massachusetts

Monday, October 1, 1973
Feast of St. Romanos the Melodist

CHAPTER ONE

Liturgical Living

The Significance of Being Christian

Did you ever ask yourself if your life has any real purpose? There are many people today, philosophers and scholars, as well as plain ordinary people who think that men and women really have no ultimate purpose, that our existence is a biological accident, that life as we experience it is a flash in the void, both temporary and without meaning or purpose.

Christians, who believe in God as Creator cannot hold such a pessimistic view of man. Christians understand that man is really the end result of God's creative action. Regardless of the process by which mankind came into existence, the Scriptures teach that mankind's destiny and purpose is to become "perfect as our Father in heaven is perfect" and that our ultimate goal and purpose as individuals and as a people is to be "the image and the likeness of God."

On the one hand then, the Orthodox Christian faith sees for each and every human being a wonderful and inspiring purpose in life: to become as much as is humanly possible like God. This happens when our thoughts are like His thoughts, our desires coincide with His desires, our will chooses as He chooses, our actions are reflections of His actions. In other words, we become like God when our ways of thinking, feeling, acting, and doing are united with God's ways of doing these things. We fulfill our purpose as human beings when we are thus united with God. Certainly, this is a glorious and wonderfully inspiring destiny and purpose that you and I and all persons have! Our life on earth then has great meaning and significance: to develop and to grow little by little into that image and likeness of God. In other words it simply means that we are to become as fully human as possible!

Yet, we all know that things are not that simple. Human beings do not grow in a natural, even and unobstructed way toward the fulfillment of that union with God and the realization of their own human potential. We can expect that if we plant a lily bulb, with a minimum of proper care, the bulb in due time will sprout and soon present us with its lovely trumpet-like flowers in an almost automatic fashion. Not so with man. Something seems to prevent that natural and easy growth. It is as if there is some perverse force which causes us again and again to separate ourselves from thinking and desiring and willing, and acting in a God-like way. The name we give to this separation between the ways we actually act and the ways which our purpose and destiny require us to act, is "sin."

Sin *means* not being united with God, that is, not living like God and thus not fulfilling our purpose as human beings. This perverse condition of sin seems to have a very profound influence in our lives. We have discovered that if we try to overcome this separation by ourselves, we always fail. In the Old Testament story of Adam and Eve, the reason for this is described to us. In that story we are told that Adam and Eve "chose" to disobey God. The result of that choice was expulsion from the Garden. We were separated from God and the way which God would have us act. The story points to the fact that mankind's thoughts and desires and will and actions are not anymore united with those of God. Men and women are not only separated from God, but they are also separated from their own true self, since their true self exists and can be realized only when they are united with God.

This then leads us inexorably to affirm a paradoxical truth; men and women are really *less than human*! We are not, really, truly, fully, human because we are not united with God, nor even growing into that union, which, as we saw above, means thinking and desiring and willing and acting like God. Our minds are darkened; our desires oftentimes perverted; our wills weak; and our actions are disoriented. The practical consequence of this state of affairs is that we go wrong. We often do evil things and we frequently fail to do the good things which we ought to do. The name we give to this condition of separateness from God is "original sin." As long as we are in this condition of original sin we are not able to bridge the gap ourselves. As much as we try, we are not able any more, on our own initiative, to overcome the separation between our present-selves and our true-selves, between ourselves as we are (really less than human) and ourselves as we ought to be (like God or fully human).

No matter what we do, we cannot pull ourselves up out of the quicksand of this condition of separation from God. But God can reach out and extend the hand of salvation to us! He is not obligated to do so, to be sure. Yet, that is exactly what He did. He made the first move to re-unite Himself with men and women, to give them again the possibility of being united with Him. He acted so as to give us the possibility of acting and desiring and willing and acting as God acts.

We call this generous outreach of God for our redemption and salvation "Divine Grace" and He has shown that Grace in many ways. The most important way was through His Son, Jesus Christ. The whole meaning of Christ's Incarnation, Death, and Resurrection is that we are given the opportunity again to realize our potential and purpose as human beings. One of the Fathers of the Church has written that "God became Man so that we could become gods." Christ through His death took the brunt of the spiritual death which we were living upon Himself. His Death and Resurrection restored the possibility to every man to live and think and desire and will as God does. Growth is to follow. Thus St. Paul writes in his letter to the Ephesians, "We are to grow in every way into Him who is the Head, into Christ." And the Apostle Peter instructs, "grow in the grace and knowledge of our Lord and Saviour Jesus Christ." We are, in St. Paul's phrase, "predestined to be conformed to the image of His Son."

Of course, to grow means that we must enter into a struggle to overcome the habitual and practical aspects of our separation from God. This is why so many of the Fathers of the Church emphasize the need for continuous and constant repentance as a part of our Christian life. One modern writer describes repentance in this fashion:

> Repentance is a condition which should continue always. It is the constant position of those who truly desire their union with God . . . Repentance means that I regret every sin and violation of God's law which I have committed . . . It is a turning from darkness to light, from the dominance of Satan to the sovereignty of God, that we "may receive forgiveness of sins and a place among those who are consecrated" (Acts 26:18). Repentance, then, is a continuous going out from our own self which is under the influence of sin. It is a power which activates the transformation of our nature.

The struggle to grow, which is most characterized by the continuous repentance of the Christian is aided by many other practices of the Christian life. Fasting with sincere intent is one of the chief means in living our struggle for growth. Necessary also, are a regular prayer life, regular worship and doing works of love. These and other practices help us grow in the image and the likeness of God.

This life of *askesis* or spiritual exercise is needed because we still share, in part, in the life which is not in full and perfect communion with God. Yet in spite of that, we must also keep before us the fact that our basic situation has changed. Something very important has happened to us because of what Christ has done; something, which—in spite of our failings and sins—means that we are no longer strangers to God, no longer foreign to Him, no longer outsiders. Through our Baptism we have entered into His household; we have been adopted as sons and daughters; we are now no longer citizens under the reign of death and sin and evil. We are citizens of the heavenly Father's Kingdom!

Our change from one condition to the other can be likened to the experience of a person who was in great danger of losing his life and was unexpectedly saved.

It is as if we were sinking in quicksand, separated from any hope of salvation and God extended a hand to us through what His Son Jesus Christ did. By accepting that extended hand we begin to be lifted out of that sure death. Even before we are out of it and cleansed of its slime, we rejoice because we know that as long as we grasp hold of that hand we are saved. Accepting the saving hand of Jesus Christ, being united with Him in that unbroken handclasp is what it means to simply *be* a Christian. Accepting for yourself that Christ's redemptive work, His teaching, and life, and death and resurrection apply to you, restoring basic communication and union between yourself and God and your present self with your true self is what we call "Faith" or "belief."

But that faith and belief is not offered to us as an option and choice in a vacuum. It is not just you and Jesus Christ facing each other. There is the multitude of humanity involved. Many have accepted that offered hand of Jesus Christ, and since He is no longer here in the flesh to offer it to you, that saving assistance of God is offered to you through the body of those who have already been lifted up into the road of salvation. Those throughout the centuries who have believed and accepted what Christ has done and who have been granted the presence of the Holy Spirit and who have witnessed the saving power and love and forgiveness of the Holy Trinity, make up that body. Throughout the ages we have called that body, "The Church."

The Church does many things: it preaches and teaches the word of God to all men and women—and it thus continues the saving teaching work of Jesus Christ. It guides men and women in their spiritual growth and administers the spiritual life of the Christians—thus continuing as well as pointing to the Lordship of Christ over the faithful and the world. The Church is also the agent which mediates the saving acts of Jesus Christ to individuals and the body of believers. It also embodies their response to God. In this, the Church continues the saving work of Christ as it was expressed on the Cross, in His Resurrection and His Ascension. The means by which Jesus Christ's saving help is made available to you and the primary means by which you, together with all the other members of the Church, respond to that action of God are the *mysteria* or "Sacraments" of the Church.

The Sacramental or "Mystical" Life

We are received into the body of the Church through Baptism in which we reject the ways of sin and separation from God and join ourselves to Christ. When we are joined to Christ, we are freed from the condition of separation from God. Once baptized, we have the potential again, with the help of God, to begin growing into the "image of God." Once baptized, nothing holds us back anymore from realizing our human potential to become what we ought to be, to become—regardless of how you prefer to phrase it—"like God" or "fully human." The condition of separation between God and man which we call "original sin" is overcome. The Sacrament of Baptism is the way that God's saving action is made available to each and every human being; and the Sacrament of Baptism is the way we respond to what God has done for us. In Baptism God stretches out His hand to us; and by being baptized we grasp that hand.

Naturally, Baptism is just the beginning of the road of Christian growth. There is need for education and training. We must struggle to overcome sinful tendencies. We will use many different means to help us grow into that image of God which we are destined to realize. Prayer, fasting, devotional practices such as the "Jesus Prayer," the reading of scripture and other spiritual books, the overcoming of vices and the development of virtues, as well as increasing our expressions of love for God and our fellowman, are essential aspects of being a Christian. But they are all part of an already real "Christian Life." As Christians we are marked as ones who belong to God because of our Baptism and as a consequence we have entered into a pattern of growth and spiritual development.

The rest of the Sacraments or Mysteria are the con-

18

tinuation of that pattern as we begin to grow more and more fully into the image of God. The Sacrament of Chrismation, which in the Orthodox Church is nearly always joined to the Sacrament of Baptism, provides us with the gift of the seal of the Holy Spirit. If Baptism cleared the way for our growth, Chrismation gives us the necessary positive emphasis for that growth to commence and to begin to realize the presence of the Holy Spirit. That is why already baptized converts are received into the Church through Chrismation usually. The Sacraments of Holy Orders (Ordination of Clergymen); Matrimony; Unction (healing of bodily and spiritual ills) and Penance (forgiveness of sins committed after Baptism) apply to specific aspects of the Christian life.

In the case of Ordination, the Holy Spirit completes and strengthens those who have been selected to serve the Church as Deacons, Priests, and Bishops. In the case of Holy Matrimony, the union of man and woman as husband and wife is sanctified and blessed with the gift of the Holy Spirit creating a new entity—"the Church in the home." In the case of Holy Unction our physical and spiritual ills and infirmities are subjected to God's healing grace and presence. In the case of the Sacrament of Penance or Holy Confession our failures and our backsliding on the road of growth in the image and likeness of God receive forgiveness, correction and guidance. Through the Sacraments we gain direction and impetus in the Christian life.

In each of these Sacraments we both give and receive. By presenting ourselves to God for His Grace and blessing in these Sacraments, we admit we need His aid and assistance and presence. We also celebrate the presence of God's Holy Spirit brought to us through the Sacraments. In the Sacrament "the Spirit helps us in our weakness."

The one Sacrament, together with Baptism, however, which covers the whole dimension of our Christian existence is the Sacrament variously known as the "Holy Eucharist," "Holy Communion," "The Mystical Banquet," and the "Lord's Supper." Its unique place in the life of Orthodox Christians is seen in the fact that it is the central and primary act of worship for the Church, since it is conducted each Sunday and on other days for and by the whole congregated body of Christians in each parish.

In this Sacrament we especially see the significance of what it means to be a member of the Church; what it means to grow in the image and likeness of God; what it means to love God and our fellow men; and what it means to receive the continuing presence of the Holy Spirit in our lives. In the Sacrament of the Holy Eucharist, especially as participants in Holy Communion, we receive the Divine Presence in our lives in the most realistic of ways and we affirm our union and desire to be one in thought and desire and will and action with God.

By uniting ourselves with God through the Sacraments and through them receiving His gracious presence and by responding to it we live the "Sacramental Life" or the "Mystical life in Christ." Essentially the Sacramental life is the primary means by which the Christian's life is united with God. On the one hand, the Sacramental Life brings to us Divine Grace, the active energy and presenc; of God which raises and strengthens us for the task of fulfilling the image and likeness of God in our lives. On the other, the Sacramental life is one of main expressions of our reaction to what God has done for us. When we participate in the Sacraments we affirm that we are "a chosen race, a royal priesthood, a holy nation, God's own people." The whole cycle of worship in the Church, however, is more than the reception of Grace and the response of a grateful people. This is especially true of the Sacraments. Our Sacramental life is a "living reality full of 'mystical presence,' which is renewed and continued for our sake in the Divine Liturgy, in the other sacraments, in the feasts of the Church year and in the various Church services." The author of these lines, University of Athens Professor of Theology Evangelos D. Theodorou, notes further that through the sacramental life in the Orthodox Church, "we are crucified with Christ, we are buried with Him, we are resurrected with Him and 'we sit with him in heavenly places' (Ephesians 2:6). It is especially through Holy Communion that the faithful are mystically united with Christ, becoming 'one in body', and 'one in blood' and 'Christ-bearers' and 'God-bearers'. Thus, the fully conscious living of the content of our Orthodox worship means nothing other than our participation in the mystical life of Christ and in the rich blessings which flow out of the redemptive work of the Lord." When the Sacraments are the locus of our relationship with God, the place where unity with God and growth in His image are focused, we are then living Sacramentally and mystically.

Many years ago, in the fourteenth century, a Bishop of Thessalonica, Nicholas Cabisilas, wrote about the Sacramental life in a book entitled *The Life In Christ*. In this book he called the Sacraments "The Gates of Heaven" and he spoke of them in the following impressive manner.

Those who become participants in the Sacraments are reborn and recreated spiritually and in a unique and exceptional way are joined and united with the Savior. This wonderful action of the Sacrament is what St. Paul had in mind when he preached on Mars Hill to the Athenians that "in Him we live and move and have our being" (Acts 17:28). And truly Baptism gives to man his existence and life in Christ. The Sacrament receives a man who is distorted by sin and spiritually dead and it introduces him to the "new", the spiritual, the Christ-like life. Chrismation, which follows immediately after baptism grants to the newly baptized gifts and energies which are necessary for the life in Christ. The Holy Eucharist maintains·and supports this spiritual life and health, for the "Bread of life" gives us the power to always remain on this higher level of living. Thus, through the Holy Eucharist, we live; through Chrismation we move and act, once we received our spiritual existence in the beginning through Baptism.

The Sacramental life is thus at the heart of what it means to be a Christian. But, as we have seen, the most inclusive and overarching of the Sacraments is the Holy Eucharist. In this book our interest is to learn how this Sacramental attitude can be most effectively and practically realized in reference to the Holy Eucharist as it is conducted in the Divine Liturgy of St. John Chrysostom.

21

We seek to discover specifically how the Divine Liturgy can for the urban, educated, twentieth-century Orthodox Christian become in conscious reality an important, vital, life-giving and life-expressing experience. In order for the Sacrament of the Holy Eucharist to become truly meaningful both as a source of Grace and as our response to that gift, as well as a sign of our membership in God's Kingdom, we must briefly turn our attention now to the understanding the Church has of the Eucharist itself. In other words, we must obtain a clear understanding of the Orthodox Church's Doctrine of the Sacrament of the Holy Eucharist.

The Church's Teaching About the Sacrament of the Eucharist

The Divine Liturgy is the way the Orthodox Church conducts the *Mystery* or Sacrament of the Holy Eucharist. There are several forms of the Divine Liturgy in the Orthodox Church, but the most common is the Divine Liturgy of St. John Chrysostom. It is conducted according to the practice of the Church on practically every Sunday in the Church calendar, as well as on weekday Feasts.

What is the Sacrament of the Eucharist, then? It certainly is more than the specific forms or the exact hymns which are sung in a particular order. As we have seen, it is a Sacrament which is closely related to what it means to be a Christian and a member of the Orthodox Church. There is no need to present a detailed and exhaustive account of the Church's teaching about the Sacrament of the Eucharist for you at this time. It is enough to point to a few of the most important elements of that doctrine as they specifically apply to our efforts to learn how to participate in the Divine Liturgy.

The Sacrament had its beginning with the Last Supper which Christ shared with His disciples before His betrayal and crucifixion. Much was said and done during that event which is of great interest to us. "And as they were eating, Jesus took bread, and blessed it, and brake it, and gave it to the disciples, and said, Take, eat, this is my body. And He took the cup, and gave thanks, and gave it to them saying, Drink of it ye all; for this is my blood of the New Testament, which is shed for many for the remission of sins." This passage, and several more like it affirm one of the most essential aspects of the Sacrament; that in a mystical yet real manner, the Bread and Wine we receive in the Sacrament are the *Body and Blood of our Lord.* In fact, in the Gospel of John the absolute necessity of this Sacrament of the Body and Blood of Christ for the Christian life is strongly emphasized. Jesus answered persons who questioned the reality of the Body and Blood in the Sacrament with the following words, "Verily, verily, I say unto you, except ye eat the flesh of the Son of man, and drink His blood, ye have no life in you. Whoso eateth my flesh, and drinketh my blood, hath eternal life; and I will raise him up at the last day. For my flesh is meat indeed, and my blood is drink indeed. He that eateth my flesh, and drinketh my blood, dwelleth in me, and I in him."

The results of taking into ourselves the Body and Blood of Christ are many. "The first and most important [is] the *unity of the believer with Christ* and the subsequent increase of the new life of grace which arises and is maintained through it" says theologian Panagiotes Trembelas. The same author points to the fact that frequent participation in the Sacrament of Holy Communion aids in weakening our tendencies to sin and in *increasing our growth* in the true and abundant life. The Sacrament is also a *source of forgiveness* of sins which are not great enough to bar us from Communion as unworthy participants.

Professor Trembelas also notes that "if each of us is united with Christ through the Holy Eucharist it is evident that through Christ all are united to each other." The Body and Blood of Christ not only unites us to God but also unites us *to our fellow Christians.* St. John of Damascus expresses that truth when in commenting on the word "communion" he says that the Sacrament is called communion not only because we commune with Christ, but also because "through it we commune with and are united with one another. For because we all receive from one bread, one Body of Christ and one Blood, we become members of one another—all together one body with Christ." This is important when we consider that the Service of the Liturgy through which the Sacrament is conducted serves to realize and express our unity as Christians. In addition, the Body and Blood of Christ points to and begins to realize the future dimensions of our existence in Christ. The Sacrament as conducted in the Liturgy is an act on the part of the Church which expresses and realizes its own reality before God. At its heart the Liturgy, in the words of one theologian is "the Church's act of self-revelation, self-fulfillment, self-expression." In the Eucharistic Liturgy *we are more than ever the Church* proclaiming its unity with Christ, its own internal corporateness and its identity with the Church of history and the Church which goes beyond history, the Eternal Kingdom of God. Further, Holy Communion, in the understanding of the Fathers, is also "a *medicine of immortality,* an antidote to death, leading to life in Jesus Christ, forever." It points to the fact that the Sacrament both verifies our present membership in God's Eternal Kingdom and assures that eternal life in the future.

In addition, there is another aspect of the Eucharist, *its sacrificial character.* In the Sacrament of the Eucharist, Christ is offered as a sacrifice on our behalf to God. The Sacrament is a bloodless offering of the very same Body and Blood offered once and for all by Christ on the Cross. That one sacrifice is offered in each parish Church, with each congregation sharing in the offering of it and contributing to it, through their gifts of bread and wine, through their participation in the praise and glory offered to God and their reception of the effects of Christ's redeeming sacrifice in Sacramental Communion. The Fathers of the Church insist that there is only one sacrifice—that of Christ on the cross. The Sacramental Sacrifice in the Eucharist, performed in every parish Church over and over again is an "individualization" of that one sacrifice, not a new or different one. Theodoritus, a 5th century Syrian Bishop, says that "the priests of the New Testament who conduct the Mystical liturgy do not offer it as a different sacrifice, but rather commemorate that One sacrifice" so that "they have no need of any other." Thus, in the Sacrament of the Eucharist we have not only the very Body and very Blood of Christ, but also the real redemptive sacrifice of Christ, realized and made particular for each and every Christian in attendance. It is in this manner that the Orthodox Church understands Christ's words, "Do this, as often as you drink it, in remembrance of me," in that St. Paul adds, "For as often as you eat this bread and drink the cup, you proclaim the Lord's death until He comes."

In this sacrifice, as performed in the Divine Liturgy, we thank God for His blessings ("Eucharist" means "thanksgiving"), we appeal to Him in our petitions, and we offer it on behalf of the whole world, living and dead, for whom Christ died.

The sacrificial character of the Holy Eucharist also leads to the inclusion of elements in the Service which remind the Christian not only of Christ's redemptive death on the cross, but also of other aspects of the life of Christ.

Thus, in the Holy Eucharist we receive the Body and Blood of Christ which unites us with Christ, helps us to grow into the image and likeness of God, unites us with our fellow Christians, becomes the means by which our membership in the Kingdom of God is celebrated, mediates to us the redemptive sacrifice of Jesus Christ on the Cross, and reveals for us the whole divine and holy history of the saving life and work of Jesus Christ.

Professor Trembelas provides us with a succinct and formal definition of the Sacrament which says briefly most of the points which we have made above and with which we may conclude this short description of the Doctrine of the Sacrament of the Eucharist.

The Eucharist is that Sacrament in which Christ is truly and essentially present under the forms of bread and wine, offered as a bloodless sacrifice and a re-enactment, once and for all eternity, offered on the Cross and given as life-giving food and communion for the faithful. Thus the Eucharist has two aspects; it is on the one hand a sacrament and on the other, a sacrifice. These two equally important aspects are expressed by the many and varied names assigned by scripture and the Church's tradition to the Eucharist by which it is characterized either as a Mystery feeding the souls of the Faithful and uniting them with Christ and to one another in one bread and one body; or, as a sacrifice representing, bloodlessly and mystically, but also in reality, the sacrifice of blood on the Cross offered by the Great High Priest. Since in this Sacrament the very Body and Blood of the Lord is granted to the faithful, its superiority and special importance is evident, making it the central point to which all the other Sacraments and the whole Christian life move and about which they revolve.

Liturgical Living

We live liturgically when the Divine Liturgy is the focal point of what God does for us, as well as our reaction —as the people of God—to those acts of salvation, redemption, and sanctification. In the Divine Liturgy, we meet the real presence of Christ in the elements of the Sacrament and in the forgiving, elevating, and fulfilling presence of Christ in our lives. We do this both as individuals and as members of the Church, which is the Body of Christ. In addition, the Sacrificial character of the Liturgy mediates to us, and brings close to each of us, as individuals and as a local congregation of believers, the death and Resurrection of Christ. In the structure of the Liturgy, the Church has also seen fit to find meanings which also point to the other aspects of Christ's earthly life. The Divine Liturgy is often seen as "remembering" the whole sacrificial work of Christ from the moment of His Birth to the Ascension. The Divine Liturgy is also the place where the Church itself affirms its existence as the "people of God," where it proclaims the fact that their response to the saving work of Christ has made them members of the Kingdom of God; an experience which begins in this life and will culminate in the Eternal Kingdom. The faithful experience a foretaste of that Eternal Kingdom through the Liturgical Experience.

Further, the Church through its history has related the Divine Liturgy to the calendar. The Divine Liturgy is conducted on the "Lord's Day" ("Kyriake hemera" in Greek) which honors the Resurrection of Christ. Each day we remember a specific event in the life of Christ or the Theotokos, or we remember a Saint on the date of his or her martyrdom.

The Divine Liturgy, then, becomes the location where we are at the most intense level united with Christ and growing in the image and likeness of God. It is *the* place of "remembering" and actually sharing in the redemptive Sacrifice of Christ on the Cross, as well as His whole incarnate life. It is that action which most of all characterizes us as the Church, emphasizing our real existence as members of God's Kingdom, beginning in this life and extending into eternity. It is *the* location where time past, time present, and time future are gathered up for us in ultimate meaning and significance.

As such, the Divine Liturgy is a real, practical, experienced event which gathers together the meaning of life. To it we bring all of our concerns of life, as we shall see. When all that is important in our lives, both religiously and generally, is channelled to God and from God through the Liturgical experience, especially in the Eucharist, we "Live Liturgically."

As such, Liturgical living is a vital, vivid, vivifying reality. It is exciting and moving. It is important; one of the most important aspects of what it means to be a Christian. No more erroneous statement can be made than to assert that a person can be a "good Christian" without attending the Divine Liturgy! It is in the Divine Liturgy that we find the reality of our union with Christ and one another as the Church of God.

Real, vital, exciting, glorious, positive, real living; that is the Divine Liturgy!

27

is for some, to what it is for many today. An empirical view of the majority of our Orthodox parishes on an average Sunday morning would present us with a very mixed picture. The joy and vivacity of "Liturgical Living" is certainly not a universal phenomenon. The Divine Liturgy is conducted in a known, partially known, or unknown language as far as the communicants are concerned. One gets the impression that not all fully comprehend the significance of what is happening. The Christians in attendance (where is the rest of the "Body of Christ"?) "watch" the Service, or "follow" the Liturgy. As the Cantor or Choir sing, the congregation in most parishes stands silent and unresponsive. Though it is dangerous to judge from external appearances, much of the congregation gives the impression that they have presented themselves in a passive fashion, expecting to be "acted upon" by the Service or the sermon. Some solid parishioners convey the impression that they are in Church out of a "sense of duty." Some indicate their complete lack of comprehension and interest by staring at the ceiling and walls, and the hats on the heads of the most recent arrivals. Others maintain a whispered conversation throughout most of the Service. At best, many people attend the Divine Liturgy in a passive state in which the spirit is kept open and receptive for any chance impression or influence. At worst, for many, the Divine Liturgy is a boring and tiring experience which is "too long, irrelevant, and sooner over, the better."

Why does this contrast exist? Why is the meaningful, vital, moving and exciting real experience of "Liturgical Living" seen so rarely in our parishes?

We have already pointed out in the introduction that the *first key* which contributes to this situation is that those who do not satisfactorily participate in the Divine Liturgy usually do not have an understanding of the basic and fundamental sacramental and liturgical realities of our lives as Christians. In this Chapter we have sought to correct this lack by introducing to you the basic meaning of the Christian life, the place of the Sacraments in our lives, the essential understanding of the Doctrine of the Holy Eucharist and what it means to live Liturgically.

Yet, even if we have a full grasp of these important truths, it is not enough. What is needed in addition is to comprehend the form and structure of the Divine Liturgy. Chapter Two will help you understand the pattern of the Liturgy *to which you can bring your understanding of the Christian Life, the Sacramental Life, and Liturgical Living.*

The Living Liturgy

Even with the knowledge we have acquired, we are hard-pressed to actively participate in the Liturgy. In order to fully participate in the Divine Liturgy we must also understand its makeup and structure. There is need for you to have an over-view of the whole Divine Liturgy of St. John Chrysostom *as it is today; in the form and structure it holds in present-day Orthodox Christianity.* Throughout the Church's two thousand year history, the Divine Liturgy has developed its structure in the living experience of the Church. In this Chapter we will first trace some aspects of the development of the structure of the Divine Liturgy. We will see how this development is a mixture of both continuity and change and see how it is possible to understand the structure of the Liturgy as it is today in several ways. Finally, we will see that there is a structure to the Divine Liturgy *as it is today* that is most helpful in aiding the average Christian to participate easily and readily in the Divine Liturgy. This new understanding of the structure of the Divine Liturgy is the *second key* which will make possible your active and vital participation in the Divine Liturgy.

The Development of the Structure of the Divine Liturgy

As you remember, we said above that the Divine Liturgy is the way the Orthodox Church conducts the Sacrament of the Holy Eucharist. So, in a sense, the Sacrament itself can be distinguished from the Service by which it is performed. Today, in the Orthodox Church there are four different Divine Liturgies, but of course, only one Sacrament of the Eucharist. The Divine Liturgy of St. John Chrysostom is the most common of the Divine Liturgies. The Divine Liturgy of St. Basil is conducted only ten times during the year. In most respects, it is exactly like the Divine Liturgy of St. John Chrysostom. However, it differs from it in some of the hymns, in a few of the audible parts said by the Priest, and in many of the silent prayers. In addition to these, there is the very infrequently performed Divine Liturgy of St. James (once a year, on the Feast Day of the Saint, October 23, and then only in a few parishes). Compared to the previously mentioned Divine Liturgies this Service is very different. In content, structure, and order it is of a substantially different Liturgical tradition. Finally, there is the Divine Liturgy of the Presanctified Gifts which consists of the first part of the traditional Vesper Service and the latter part of the Divine Liturgy. In this Service, the Bread and Wine are not consecrated, for the Gifts are already "pre-sanctified" at a preceding Divine Liturgy. Thus, it is not in the full sense of the word a "Liturgy" in which the Bread and Wine are offered, consecrated and distributed. In the Pre-Sanctified Liturgy, the Holy Eucharist is only distributed. In fact, the purpose of this Service is to provide more opportunity to the faithful to receive Holy Communion during the Great Lent. For this reason, the Liturgy of the Pre-Sanctified Gifts is performed only during the Great Lent.

Even so, this Divine Liturgy of the Pre-Sanctified Gifts points to the truth that the Sacrament itself can be distinguished from the forms through which it is made available to the Faithful. This variety of present day liturgical practice also points our attention to the fact that throughout the two thousand year history of the Church the Sacrament of the Holy Eucharist has been conducted through many different forms and structures. There have been several "liturgical traditions" in the Church's history. In the paragraphs below we will touch very lightly on the liturgical tradition which finally produced the present day Services which we have in the Orthodox Church.

All of the liturgical traditions, those of Rome and

Milan, Spain and North Africa, Alexandria, and Syria, Asia Minor and Jerusalem, and that of Constantinople, have at their basis the New Testament accounts of the institution of the Sacrament as well as other elements which were included in the Eucharist in the apostolic Church. The first three Gospels, Matthew, Mark, and Luke—which are known as the Synoptic Gospels—describe the institution of the Sacrament as taking place at a Jewish Passover meal. The Fourth Gospel, the Gospel of St. John, describes it as part of a different kind of religious banquet which pious Jews at that time conducted. Such religious feasts when conducted as a domestic ceremony were known as "kiddush" and when conducted by friends as a religious social meal, were known as "Chaburah." Preceding these Gospel accounts in point of time is the description by Saint Paul. These descriptions form the basis and foundation of our knowledge of the history of the Sacrament itself. They also point to some of the elements which were included from the beginning in the structure of the Service, through which the Sacrament was conducted. In the New Testament also, we find other elements which were destined to find a place in the liturgical practice of the Church such as the "Agape Meal," a religious meal which was distinct from the Sacrament, the "Kiss of Peace," the giving of alms, the recitation of prayers, the reading of Scripture passages and the explanation of those readings through a sermon, as well as the singing of hymns.

The people who study the development of the liturgical practice of the Church—known as liturgiologists—tell us that the above elements all existed from the very beginning, but in a loose and not well defined form. At the beginning, the bishop of the local congregation appears to have put together these various elements as he saw fit. Later, some writers suggested patterns which should be followed. Apparently these reflected the practices with which they were familiar. Thus, sometime between the years 100 and 130 A.D. an anonymous author wrote a small book called *The Teaching of the Twelve Apostles* in which he presented a form for conducting the Holy Eucharist in which there is an emphasis on the perfection of the faithful and the gathering together of the Church into God's Kingdom, as well as references to the Eucharist as a sacrifice.

About the year 95 A.D. Clement, a Bishop of Rome, in a letter to the Church in Corinth, suggests that certain ideas and formal phrases had already taken their place in the devotional practices of the Church. His letter shows that there existed a definite pattern to which the leaders of Church worship more or less conformed. The Roman philosopher-administrator Pliny, in writing to the Emperor Trajan about the Christians in the year 112 A.D., informs us that the Christians worshipped on a fixed day of the week (Sunday) and that they sang hymns "to Christ as a god."

The first author who provides us with enough material so that we can judge what the Divine Liturgy was like from beginning to end is Justin Martyr, who wrote several works in defense of the Christian Faith. His *First Apology* was a defense of Christianity against the false accusations of the pagans and his *Dialogue With Trypho* sought to defend the new Faith against the criticisms of the Jews. If we put together the liturgical information from these two works we get the following scheme or pattern of the Divine Liturgy:

1. Readings from the Old and New Testaments.
2. A Sermon.
3. Prayers said on behalf of all men.
4. The Kiss of Peace.
5. The presentation of the Bread and the Cup (in which there is wine and water) to the leader of the Service.
6. Prayers of praise and thanksgiving offered extemporaneously over the bread and wine.
7. The administration of the elements of the Sacrament by the deacons.
8. And the collection of donations for the poor.

Justin Martyr wrote these works about the year 150 A.D.

Irenaeus, the Bishop of Lyon, writing about thirty years later mentions in his book *Against Heresies* that the offering of the bread and cup "receive the invocation of God" by which they become the Sacrament of the Eucharist. By the year 350 A.D. in Egypt, we have a sort of liturgical service book known as the *Sacramentary of Serapion* which divides the Service of the Eucharist into two parts. The first part is the Service of the "Catechumens" and the other, the Service of the offering or the "Anaphora." The Catachumens were the persons who were being instructed in the faith but who had not as yet been baptized. They were permitted to attend the first part of the Sacrament, but then were dismissed. The first part of the Divine Liturgy, then beginning to be known as the "Liturgy of the Catachumens," is described in the *Sacramentary of Serapion* as having four parts or elements:

1. The first prayer of the Trisagion (Holy God, Holy Mightly, Holy Immortal, have mercy on us . . .)
2. The Sermon.
3. Prayers after the Sermon.
4. Prayers for the Catechumens.

The second part of the Liturgy as described in this Egyptian work of the middle fourth century is the "Anaphora" or "offering." Only the faithful, baptized Christians were permitted to participate in this portion of the Divine Liturgy. From this fact it later took the name "Liturgy of the Faithful." In the *Sacramentary of Serapion* it included the following elements:

1. The Hymn "Holy, Holy, Holy, Lord God of Hosts . . . taken from the vision of the Prophet Isaiah described in the Sixth Chapter of the Old Testament book of the same name.
2. The "Anamnesis" or remembrance of the events and words by which the Sacrament of the Eucharist was founded . . . (This is my Body . . . This is my Blood . . . Do this in remembrance of me . . .).
3. The invocation or "Epiclesis" calling upon God to bless and consecrate the gifts.
4. The Commemoration of the dead.
5. The Communion.
6. The Concluding Prayers.

There is in existence a compilation of earlier materials

known as the *Apostolic Constitutions* which throughout the earlier years of the History of the Church enjoyed wide respect. In this work (which, of course, was not written by any of the Apostles but reflects the Apostolic tradition in the Church) there are two descriptions and directions for the conducting of the Sacrament of the Eucharist. The earlier one found in "Book Two" seems to belong to the third century. The second found in "Book Eight" is a fourth-century Liturgy from Antioch and is very close to the pattern and structure of the Divine Liturgy of St. John Chrysostom as we conduct it today. The Divine Liturgy as described in Book Two, no more than 170 years after Christ's Resurrection, has the following pattern or structure:

Liturgy of the Catechumens

1. Two Old Testament Readings.
2. Hymns of David with responses which came to be known as Antiphons.
3. Epistle Reading.
4. Gospel Reading.
5. Several Sermons.
6. Prayers and Dismissal of the Catechumens.

Liturgy of the Faithful

7. Deacons prepare the offerings of Bread and Wine.
8. Kiss of Peace.
9. Prayers for the Church and the World.
10. The Bishop prays for the people and for peace and then blesses the people.
11. The Sacrifice of the Body and Blood of Christ is then made.
12. The Communion.
13. The Dismissal Prayers.

As we have noted however, other specific liturgical traditions appeared geographically throughout the Christian world. Liturgical traditions peculiar to the Egyptians, the Syrians, the Romans, the Palestinians, the Africans, and others have been identified and traced in their development by liturgiologists. Finally, some generally fixed patterns appear to have remained fairly stable over the past fifteen hundred years. Yet, even today, in the liturgical tradition of the Eastern Orthodox Church, we find slow changes. For all practical purposes, in many jurisdictions of the Orthodox Church, for instance, the ancient prayers for the Catechumens are no longer said, nor are the Psalms said at the antiphons in many jurisdictions.

Continuity and Change

This change and development in the structure of the Liturgy raises a question for the Orthodox believer. We have been taught that the Orthodox Church has maintained unchanged the teaching and practices and traditions of the ancient undivided Church. Does not the evidence we have just outlined indicate that this is not correct as far as the Divine Liturgy is concerned?

Without a doubt, the unchanging character of the traditions and practices of the Church regarding the structure of the Divine Liturgy, if understood in a literal and legalistic manner, does not correspond to fact. There have been change and development, addition and subtraction, flexibility and fluidity in the development of the Liturgy. It would be unhistorical and contrary to the living experience of the Church to argue that from the very beginning the Church conducted the Divine Liturgy exactly as we do today without the slightest alteration or development.

Yet, in a very real and essential sense, we can see that this development and fluidity have taken place within a rather narrow area. The basic New Testament and early Christian elements of the Liturgy are clearly part of the Divine Liturgy as conducted today. In fact, most of the liturgical traditions have much more in common than they do in divergence. For instance, the Latin Mass has many significant and important differences when compared to the Liturgy of St. John Chrysostom; yet, there is much more that is held in common by the two liturgical traditions, at least as far as the Service of the Holy Eucharist is concerned.

These variations in the development of the structure

of the Liturgy are unconscious reflections of the varying historical circumstances under which the Church has lived. As such, they do not reflect the essence of the tradition. These differences, by and large, are varying expressions of already existing patterns in the Divine Liturgy. For example, most of the more impressive vestments of the Bishop appeared in the worship of the Church only after the fall of the Byzantine Empire. They were adopted from the royal vestments of the Emperors of Byzantium. Even more pertinent are the prayers for the Catechumens. The earliest Liturgies did not have prayers for the Catechumens for the simple reason that the class of Catechumens as such did not exist. Later, in the third and fourth centuries when multitudes of persons sought to enter the Church, classes of instruction were organized. When the question was raised as to whether these Catechumens could attend the Divine Liturgy, a practical solution was devised. The instructional and preparatory part of the Service (Old Testament readings, New Testament readings, and Sermons) was opened to them. It was then appropriate to add special prayers on their behalf before they were dismissed. Thus, a clear "First Part" was given to the Divine Liturgy: "The Liturgy of the Catechumens." Of course, the Faithful were also in attendance during the Liturgy of the Catechumens. The "Second Part" thus naturally became known as the "Liturgy of the Faithful" during which the Bread and Wine were offered, consecrated and distributed to the baptized believers.

As we have noted however, the prayers for the Catechumens are no longer being recited in many of the Orthodox jurisdictions throughout the world. While some of the jurisdictions retain them, others have ceased to pray for the Catechumens for a very real and concrete reason: there is something inappropriate about praying to God for the welfare of a class of people who do not exist! It is equally embarrassing for the Priest or Deacon to instruct people who are not in Church to depart! Thus, though the Service books still include the prayers for the Catechumens and the Deacons are instructed to say,

"Let all of the Catechumens depart," in many Churches these rubrics are skipped over without any sense of guilt, but rather with a feeling of intrinsic honesty since they have no real meaning any more.

The purpose of this and the preceding section has been to point to the fact that though there have been change and development in the structure and the make-up of the Divine Liturgy, there has also been an essential continuity. In a very real sense, the essence of the Divine Liturgy in all ages has been the same. All of the elements which existed in the ancient New Testament tradition are found in every age and at present. The changes which have taken place throughout two thousand years of history are remarkably few in number and small in extent. The essential pattern of the Divine Liturgy of St. John Chrysostom, as we have seen above, was already a part of the *Apostolic Constitutions* in the fourth century. The additions and changes which have taken place since then in no way detract from the fact that almost total continuity and identity have been maintained in the liturgical forms of the Church since that time. We are certainly justified then, in saying that the Divine Liturgy is essentially unchanged from the beginning. Yet, we are also justified in noting that there is no particular halo on any specific way of looking at the makeup of the Divine Liturgy as it stands today. Though in its present form, the Divine Liturgy has a very stable and concrete form there is nothing that requires us to look at that form in terms of its divisions and parts in only one way. In fact there are many ways that it can and has been done. To these we now turn our attention.

Patterns and Structures of the Divine Liturgy

The Divine Liturgy of St. John Chrysostom has had a development throughout its history so that at various points in that development it could have been divided differently. For instance, at one time in its history the Bread and Wine were prepared during the course of the Liturgy itself. Known technically as the "Liturgy of the

Oblation" it can be seen, for example, as step five in the liturgical scheme of Justin Martyr which we described above. As such, we have the following "parts" of the Divine Liturgy:

1. Liturgy of the Catechumens.
2. Liturgy of the Oblation.
3. Liturgy of the Faithful.

Later, however, the "Liturgy of the Oblation" was lifted out of its place in the middle of the Service and placed at the very beginning, becoming in the process a non-public and inaudible part of the Divine Liturgy. Known also as the "Proskomide" (meaning "offering" from the Greek word "proskimizo") it now is thought of as a preliminary to the Divine Liturgy which could not be performed without it. Today, many persons, in describing the structure of the Divine Liturgy present the following pattern:

1. Proskomide (Liturgy of Oblation)
2. Liturgy of the Catechumens.
3. Liturgy of the Faithful.

And, of course, many handbooks to the Divine Liturgy for the benefit of the Faithful tend to ignore the Proskomide and thus divide the Divine Liturgy into just the Liturgy of the Catechumens and the Liturgy of the Faithful. However, other authors, recognize that a division of the Service on these lines is no longer realistic (since there are no Catechumens as a separate class anymore). They have sought other practical and useful divisions of the material of the Liturgy in order to aid the contemporary Orthodox Christian in participating in the services. For example, in the well-known book by Timothy Ware, *The Orthodox Church,* the author divides the Divine Liturgy into (I) The Office of Preparation, (II) The Liturgy of the Word (Opening Service, The Little Entrance, Readings from Scripture, Intercession for the Church), and (III) The Eucharist (Great Entrance, Kiss of Peace and Creed, The Eucharistic Prayer, the Elevation and Fraction, Communion, Conclusion). He thus avoids the terminology which refers to "Catechumens" and "Faithful." There are presently, in America, for instance, a large number of Divine Liturgy handbooks, each of which makes some kind of arbitrary division in the Divine Liturgy. For instance, in the Greek Archdiocese alone, Fathers Elias, Theodore, Papadeas, Kallelis, and Makris, among others, have presented Liturgy Handbooks divided in various ways. All of these books include very interesting and useful aids to the concerned worshipper. Some have fine illustrations, some have detailed descriptions of liturgical acts, some have the Scripture Readings for the year, others are rich in explanatory notes. None, however, in attempting to structure the Divine Liturgy has done it so as to guide the Orthodox Worshipper consistently and concretely in specific acts of participation.

What would such a division of the structure of the Divine Liturgy have to do? First of all, a division of practical use for direct participation in the Divine Liturgy would have to reflect the present reality of the absence of a class of Catechumens. In a sense, we are all in the process of learning and growing in the Faith; in a sense, we are all "catechumens." But as baptized members of the Church we attend the Divine Liturgy from the beginning through to the end. The divisions cannot be in touch with reality if they assume that some of us leave at the middle of the Service! A realistic division of the parts of the Divine Liturgy then will see it as a whole, divided into its respective parts.

Secondly, a contemporary and relevant division of the Divine Liturgy must be grounded in the very liturgical forms of the Divine Liturgy. If we can discover a certain pattern in the makeup of the Divine Liturgy which uses the liturgical forms in a rational and intelligent manner, we will have justification and guidance in working out these divisions. Such a pattern grounded in the forms of the Divine Liturgy of St. John Chrysostom exists.

Thirdly, each of the segments which we identify should be readily identifiable as to its purpose and function in the whole movement of the Divine Liturgy. If this is the case—and it is—then each of the segments which we seek to identify becomes a "unit" with its own purpose, content, and goal. Each "unit" then is a portion of the Divine Liturgy which allows our conscious and active participation. And finally, such a division should reflect the makeup of all of the rest of the other Services of the Orthodox Church. It should be a division which finds parallels in the rest of the liturgical Services of the Church.

Thus, a realistic and practical division of the Divine Liturgy whose purpose it is to concretely assist the modern Orthodox Christian in participating in the Divine Liturgy would (1) take into consideration that the Divine Liturgy today is attended almost exclusively by baptized Christians from beginning to end. (2) It should be based on the very liturgical makeup of the Divine Liturgy as it is today. (3) The method should divide the Divine Liturgy into practical "units" which assist the worshipper in consciously and actively participating in the Liturgy. (4) Finally, it should reflect the pattern of Orthodox Worship generally. Such a division of the Divine Liturgy of St. John Chrysostom exists within its very makeup and structure.

The Nine Sections of the Divine Liturgy

As we saw above, the practical need to instruct English-speaking converts led to the development of the method of liturgical participation presented in this book. However, it is closer to the truth to say that the need would never have been met if it were not for a chance suggestion by an English writer on Orthodoxy and a vexing question about some repetitions in the Divine Liturgy. The English writer was R. M. French, in his little introductory book *The Eastern Orthodox Church*. This author presents, for English readers, a general account of the history, beliefs, worship, and practices of the Orthodox Church. In the section on "Worship" French sought to explain the unique structure of Orthodox Services to his readers. In his discussion of the Services, he explains the nature of the Orthodox hymn and its place in the

Services, showing "that nearly 80% of the Services consist of hymns which are not at all like the hymns in western Church usage. They are rhythmical compositions in poetical language. A general name which covers a large number of them is *troparion* (Slavonic: *tropar*), and the Orthodox Services are festooned with them, strung together with *Glorias* and broken verses from the psalms *"like pearls on a string."* The important phrase in his description for our purposes is the phrase "like pearls on a string." The Vespers and the Orthros (Matins) can be described readily with that phrase. For instance, the hymns before the Entrance (Stichera) and after the Entrance (Aposticha) of the Vesper Service can easily be thought of in this manner. However, this same idea of "pearls on a string" can also be applied to the Divine Liturgy. Not, to be sure, to the individual hymns, but to the *sections* which make up the Divine Liturgy. If one could discern a pattern, a structure, a makeup to the Liturgy, providing units of conprehension, he would have the image of the Divine Liturgy much like a pearl pendant!

But how are we to discern these "pearls" of the Divine Liturgy? Several authors have made arbitrary headings for the practical use of the faithful in popular "Liturgy Books." Yet, that is exactly what they were, arbitrary divisions, which were not, in reality, reflecting the Divine Liturgy's own makeup and built-in pattern.

The idea suggested by French that the Services of the Orthodox Church have a pattern "like pearls strung on a string" found its fruition in and suggested an answer to one of the most frequently voiced questions heard in reference to the Divine Liturgy: "Why is there such a frequent repetition of the Shorter Litany in the Divine Liturgy?" This Litany, which is repeated quite frequently in the Divine Liturgy, is as follows:

Celebrant: Again and again, in peace let us pray to the Lord.
Choir: Lord, have mercy.
Celebrant: Help, save, be merciful and protect us, O God, by thy grace.
Commemorating our most holy, pure, blessed, and

glorified Lady, Mother of God, and Ever-Virgin Mary, with all the Saints, let us commend ourselves and one another and our whole life to Christ, our God.

Choir: To Thee, O Lord.

Celebrant: For Thou art Holy and to Thee we ascribe glory (Note that this ascription regularly changes, but that the continuation invariably remains the same) to the Father, and the Son, and to the Holy Spirit, now and forever and unto ages of ages. Amen.

Liturgical scholars, in discussing this Shorter Litany, point out that the final part with its changing ascription may have been at one time in the development of the Divine Liturgy the final part of prayers said by the celebrant which are now no longer said audibly. Most of these prayers have become the inaudible prayers said by the Priest during the singing of the hymns of the Divine Liturgy. That means that in the vast majority of cases the prayer is actually said *after* the ascription is heard in the Shorter Litany. It has little or no bearing on the present structure of the Liturgy.

But, from a practical point of view, if you join the concept of the structure of the Divine Liturgy "like pearls on a string" with the frequent repetition of the Shorter Litany, you are immediately led to a realization that *the Shorter Litanies serve to divide the Divine Liturgy into distinctly indentifiable units.*

Further examination shows that each shorter Litany serves as the *end-point* and conclusion of each of these units or sections. They stand as a kind of signal-flag, attracting attention to the fact that the section has come to an end.

In content, the shorter Litany is like the theme of a Symphony. Just as a symphonic theme is repeated over and over again in many variations, the shorter Litany appears in many different, yet clearly recognizable forms throughout the Divine Liturgy. And each time that it does so, it serves to signal the end of a clearly defined portion of the Divine Liturgy. Each of these portions has a readily identifiable intent and purpose in the movement of the Divine Liturgy. This provides a clear point of reference for understanding not only what is going on in the Divine Liturgy, but also for comprehending what is required to participate actively and consciously in the Service. Thus, for purposes of actual participation (not academic theorizing) the Divine Liturgy *as conducted today* and for the *kind of Christians we are today*, is seen as a series of sections or "pearls." Each section is complete in itself, fulfilling its own purpose. But like the single pearl in a pearl pendant, it adds to the whole, so that the whole is more beautiful, more meaningful, and richer than the sum of its parts.

This approach to the Divine Liturgy helps the average Christian see the Divine Liturgy as composed of a number of "units" to which he is able to give his attention. He is not overwhelmed at once by the richness and wealth of the liturgical pattern of the whole Divine Liturgy. Educators have long known that people learn much better and faster if the year's material is broken down into units of study. In the same manner, worship is facilitated, made easier to understand and given immediate relevance, when its parts are identified as to their purpose and significance. The worshipper then truly knows what he is doing; he really "understands" what is going on. And he therefore has the necessary presupposition for actual active and personal *participation* in the Divine Liturgy.

If, then, we go through the Divine Liturgy, looking for the shorter Litanies and noting where they stand in reference to the rest of the liturgical material, how many sections (units?) (pearls?) do we discover? We discover that there are nine such clearly defined sections in the Divine Liturgy. Some are short; some are long. Each of the shorter Litanies has its own modification and variation. Yet, even a quick review of the Divine Liturgy on the basis of what we have said above provides this pattern of the makeup of the Divine Liturgy of Saint John Chrysostom:

1. Litany.
2. First Antiphon.
3. Second Antiphon.

4. Third Antiphon (Little Entrance).
5. Scripture Readings.
6. Great Entrance.
7. Great Eucharistic Prayer (Anaphora).
8. Communion.
9. Dismissal.

We will, in subsequent chapters, examine these sections word by word, with the intent of showing the Orthodox Christian how he or she can specifically participate in each of these units of the Divine Liturgy. We thus have before us the second "key" for participating in the Divine Liturgy. The first was the understanding of the Sacrament itself and of Sacramental Living. The second key, which we have seen in this chapter, is the "unit" or "section" approach to the structure of the Divine Liturgy. It has pointed you to the fact that the Divine Liturgy of the Orthodox Church is neither static nor monolithic. It has brought you one step closer to real, vital, and personal participation by showing to you the makeup and structure of "The Living Liturgy."

CHAPTER THREE

Living the Liturgy

Introduction

In the previous Chapters we pointed to the need for three essential requirements if the Divine Liturgy were to become for us a living, powerful, and moving experience.

The first need is to understand what the Divine Liturgy is. We said simply that it is the way the Orthodox Church performs the Holy Eucharist. The Holy Eucharist is that Sacrament or "Mystery" in which we receive the very Body and Blood of Christ. At the same time it is *par excellence* the event in the life of the Church which affirms her existence in the present and the future, as the people of God, His Holy nation, His earthly and heavenly Kingdom. The Divine Liturgy can never have much significance for us if this is not understood and affirmed.

The next Chapter pointed to the second essential requirement for the Divine Liturgy to become a living and vital experience for us. That was the need to understand that though the Divine Liturgy is essentially unchanged, its structure can be viewed in different ways. The present-day structure of the Liturgy can be likened to a pearl pendant which is a totality, yet is made up of individual units or sections, the individual pearls. In much the same way, we said, the Divine Liturgy *as it is structured today,* is made up of nine clearly defined sections or units. Having identified these sections, we are then in the position to grasp the purpose, significance and meaning of each unit or section of the Liturgy. The specific portion of the Liturgy before us then becomes a unit which we can understand and which speaks to us concretely and through which *we* may speak in Liturgical worship.

The third essential presupposition, which we discuss in this Chapter, is the need which the worshipping Orthodox Christian has to *actively* participate in the Divine Liturgy. It is my hope in this Chapter to show you, first, why it is proper for lay people to participate in the Liturgy, and secondly, the various ways lay people can participate in the Service.

The Laity in the Church

It is important for us to note briefly the place of the laity in the Church so that we can see that lay-participation is an essential and real element in the whole action and drama of the Liturgy.

The basis of the place of the laity in the Church is the doctrine of the Unity of the Church. The Church is One. That Unity is most often thought of by the Orthodox in these days of ecumenical discussion as an affirmation which sets off the Orthodox from the other Churches. Yet, by saying the Church is One we also point to the unity of its inner life. If the Church, the people of God, are one they all share equally in the same experience and reality of their condition before God.

The Apostle Timothy refers to this reality of the Church as "the household of God." The household has its unity first and then only can we speak of distinctions such as those of parents and children. St. Paul uses the famous image of the body to express the same truth in his letters to the Christians in Ephesus and Colossae. The Body of the Church is a totality, a unity, before we begin to distinguish its members. How did we become this body? St. Paul tells us in the twelfth chapter of 1 Corinthians: "By one Spirit we were baptized into one body . . ." and thus . . . "you are the body of Christ and individually members of it." St. Basil pointed to the same truth when he said, "The most important things are common to all; Baptism, salvation through faith, having God as Father, and participating in the same spirit." Elsewhere he writes:

47

Everything is equal between us (The Clergy) and you (the laity) and we have the same measure of goods for I do not receive more richly and you in a lesser measure from the Holy Table, but we equally draw from it. It so happens that I go first, but this is not so great, since even among children, the oldest one extends his hand first to receive the food, but nothing more than this is done since all things are equal among us. The saving and soul-supporting (spiritual) life is given to each with the same honor. I am not one kind of sheep and you another; rather, we all share in the same thing. We have the same baptism, each of us has been made worthy of the same Spirit, each of us hurries on to the same kingdom; we are in like manner the brethren of Christ; all things are common to us!

In this and many other patristic passages, the emphasis is on our unity and equality in the reception of the grace and energy and activity of God upon us. However, there is activity directed by us to and for God also. As such, all of the members of the Church are a preisthood. The three-fold work of Christ as King and Priest and Prophet belongs in general to the whole Church. As a consequence of our baptism and Chrismation every Christian continues the saving work of Christ in some form. St. John Chrysostom writes

Thus you become king and priest and prophet in the washing (of Baptism); a king in throwing down all evil acts and destroying sin; a priest in offering yourself to God and sacrificing the body and dying to yourself; a prophet in learning of the future and being filled and sealed with zeal.

In special reference to the Divine Liturgy we are all—clergy and laymen—priests. In St. Peter's first epistle, all Christians are called to be "a holy priesthood, to offer spiritual sacrifices acceptable to God through Christ." A such we are "a chosen race, a royal priesthood, a holy nation, God's own people."

Peter Mogila, Bishop of Kiev, a writer of the 17th century, summarizing this long and extremely well documented scriptural and patristic truth of the priesthood of all Christians also clarifies the distinction inherent in this doctrine. He says, "The Priesthood is of two kinds, one is spiritual and the other sacramental. All Orthodox Christians share in the spiritual priesthood . . . and according to this priesthood offerings are made such as these: prayers, thanksgivings, mortifications of the body, a giving over to suffering for Christ's sake, and other such things." The Sacramental Priesthood is chosen and lifted up, set aside and ordained from out of the ranks of the spiritual priesthood. The Sacramental Priesthood is the main agent in the work of the Church in continuing the three-fold work of Christ. Yet, the work is that of the Church, not just that of the Sacramental priesthood. The work of the Church is shared in by the laity—the Spiritual priesthood.

The place of the laity in fulfilling this three-fold work of the Church is richly documented in the history of the Church. In reference to the Kingly role, the laity in the past have shared in the choice and the raising up of candidates for the Sacramental Priesthood and the election of Bishops. Today they fully fulfill this role in the administration of the parishes.

The laity have always shared in the teaching or Prophetic role of the Church. Lay teachers are characteristic of the Orthodox from the time of Origen. This is seen in the Monastic teaching traditions, in the predominance of lay Theologians and today, even in the lay-taught Sunday School.

Regarding the High-Priestly role, it is common knowledge that the presence of laymen at all Sacraments is a necessary condition for their performance. A Priest may not properly conduct the Divine Liturgy alone, for there are no "private masses" in the Orthodox Liturgical rubrics. This, because the whole Church conducts the Sacrament. Certainly the Priest in his full priestly and sacerdotal power theoretically may do so, but the spirit of the Church's organic unity prohibits this in practice. The laity share in the Eucharist not only as receivers of the consecrated Body and Blood, but from ancient times, as those who offer the bread and wine, and who, in the words of Mogila quoted above, exercise their priesthood with prayers and thanksgiving in the Liturgy. It is only the most recent editions of the liturgical texts which describe the liturgical dialogue as taking place between Priest and Choir. All the ancient texts from their earliest form always refer to Priest and *"Laos,"* that is the Laity, the people. The word "Liturgy" itself means "a work of the people" ("Leitourgia" is made up of two Greek words "laos" and "ergon" which means "work"). From pre-Christian times "Leitourgia" has meant a service to, for and by the people.

What is the answer to the question "Who conducts the Divine Liturgy?" The answer is not "the Priest" as most would think. Nor, of course, is the answer "the people." The answer is "The Church." Of course, without the Priestly power through which Christ acts in the sacrament, there is no possibility of the fulfillment of the Mystery. But the Priest as one of the members of the Body of Christ does not function without the other members of the Body of Christ. Who then performs the Divine Liturgy? The Priest and the Laity together; the Church performs it. The sacerdotal aspect of the Service, that is, the High Priestly role, is performed by the Priest. Yet, as an essential aid and support are the prayers, thanksgivings and offerings of the laity. As members of the Body of Christ, they too both receive and call for Divine Grace. As a consequence, in order to be truly the People of God, in order to share fully in the experience of God's presence, in order to both "give their share" and "get something out of it" there is need for the laity to participate actively in the Divine Liturgy. And to this we now turn our attention.

Lay Participation in the Divine Liturgy

From all that has been said above, it should be clear that mere "following the Liturgy," mere passive physical presence, is not enough. Being there physically is a good start; but if that is all that it is, it is really of quite little value. If what is going on in Church is just a ritual form and nothing more it is not only a waste of time, it is just the opposite of true worship, it is blasphemy.

For blasphemy is the repetition of words which reflect no thoughts or feelings, affirmation or conviction. Bishop Gerasimos Papadopoulos, former Professor of New Testament at Holy Cross School of Theology in Brookline, Massachusetts, once wrote that "worship requires forms which are necessary expressions of the Spirit which underlies them—what occurs when the spirit leaves the forms is that worship loses its meaning." When the laity—out of ignorance or sloth—abandons its Spiritual Priesthood much of the Divine Liturgy loses its meaning. Certainly the Sacrament is still valid—but the Liturgy has become a kind of show, an event which Christians view and observe and to which, at best, they pay attention but do not live. No spirit underlies it, it is not the expression of *their* faith, *their* affirmation, *their* reality as the Body of Christ. In consequence the Divine Liturgy doesn't do much for them. They don't "get anything out of the Liturgy." And the reason? They don't get anything out of the Liturgy because they don't put anything into it!

If this is to be corrected, Orthodox Christians must learn to participate in the Liturgy; not as witnesses to it, but as active participants.

In the Liturgy in the 8th book of the *Constitutions of the Holy Apostles*, at the point where the Catechumens are dismissed, we have a typical set of instructions for the specific participation of the people in the Liturgy—which we note just as an example and type of what is meant:

> Ye Catechumens pray, and let *all the faithful pray for them in their mind*, saying: Lord, have mercy on them . . . (Ye Catechumens) *Bow your heads* and receive the blessing. But at the naming of everyone by the deacon as we said before, *let the people say* "Lord, have mercy on him": and let the children say it first.

Attentive participation in the Liturgy is urged in the same work, when the author describes how the faithful ought to behave in the Service:

> ". . . let the deacon oversee the people, that nobody may whisper, nor slumber, nor laugh, nor nod; for all ought in the Church to *stand wisely; and soberly, and*

attentively, having their attention fixed on the word of God.

We must now ask specifically and concretely how does one participate in the Liturgy as it is presently structured? What are the characteristics and elements of the Divine Liturgy which call forth specific kinds of response from the Orthodox Christian?

1) *Receiving Holy Communion.* Obviously, the first, primary, and most concrete manner of participation is Holy Communion. Sharing in the Mystery of the Body and Blood of Christ is the deepest, most real way of participation, if we are properly prepared. St. Cyprian writes the following important words in reference to Martyrdom, but their application to us is evident:

> We conduct the Divine Liturgy ... that we may not leave those whom we stir up and exhort to the spiritual battle unarmed and naked, but may fortify them with the protection of Christ's body and blood. And, as the Eucharist *is appointed for this very purpose*, that it be a safeguard to the receivers, it is needful that we may arm those whom we wish to be safe against the adversary with the protection of the Lord's abundance. He cannot be fitted for martyrdom who is not armed for the contest by the Church: *and his spirit is deficient which the Eucharist received does not raise and stimulate.* Communion furnishes arms to those who are about to fight.

Frequent and regular Holy Communion is vital. We cannot go Sunday after Sunday to the Divine Liturgy and ignore the invitation "With the fear of God, faith and love draw near" and think that we can be true participants in the Mystery. "Living Sacramentally" and "Living Liturgically" can never be realized in our lives if we do not receive the Body and Blood of our Lord on a frequent and regular basis. The realization of our being, as the "image and likeness of God," the presentation of ourselves as God's gathered people, the "Ecclesia" and the making real of our union with Christ will always be a truncated "half-experience" if we do not become regular communicants of the Lord's Body and Blood. In a real sense, our participation in the Divine Liturgy is not full and complete if we do not receive Holy Communion each time we attend. If that is not possible, the least which should satisfy us is to be as frequent communicants as possible. All that was said in the first chapter about the deeper meaning of the Eucharist can become a living reality for you as an individual and the parish as a community only when each Orthodox Christian becomes a frequent participant in Holy Communion. After all, Holy Communion is the chief reason for the Divine Liturgy. It is its reason for being. As we have already said: the Divine Liturgy is the way the Orthodox Church conducts the Eucharist. The Divine Liturgy is a Holy Banquet to which our Lord invites us every Sunday and Feastday. Yet, we have gotten ourselves in the practice of attending this Banquet week after week—and not sharing in it! You should not object that adequate preparation is difficult, since frequency of participation necessarily simplifies the preparation. A short fast, a simple confession, a few moments of meditation and self-examination were adequate for the early Christians. They are adequate today. Consult your Priest for specifics.

And, of course, proper preparation includes your presence and participation in the Liturgy as a worshipper as distinguished from a communicant. Even here the exercise of the Spiritual Priesthood is a necessity.

2) *Being the Church*. The Liturgy, as we have said, is not only the preparation, consecration, and distribution of the Body and Blood of Christ, it is also our affirmation of what we are: the people of God. No one has made this more clear to us Orthodox than Father Alexander Schmemann in his erudite study, *Introduction to Liturgical Theology*. In this work he shows that the "Ordo," or overall makeup of the Liturgy, "in its essential and eternal logic . . . was, is, and always will be the Ordo of the *Church's* worship, a living and vital revelation of her doctrine about herself, of her own self-understanding and self-definition." Thus, participation by the Christian in the Divine Liturgy means in part that he goes to Church *to be with* and *to be* the Church of God. There

is wisdom in the popular saying "Let's go to the Ecclesia" (Pame sten Ekklesia) rather than "Let us go to the Temple" (Naos). When we attend the Liturgy we separate ourselves from "the world" for a time. The putting aside of all worldly care is the preliminary step to participation. St. Maximos the Confessor says, "One may not worship God truly unless he fully cleanses his soul," and St. Isaias the Anchorite says, "If man does not put aside every work of this present world he may not worship God." By joyfully going to the Ekklesia we begin participation. By knowing that in the Liturgy we *are* in its fullest possible way *the Church* in this world, the new Kingdom of God, the difference and excitement and reality of the Liturgy can become real. It is no accident that the Liturgy begins with the words, "Blessed be the Kingdom of the Father and the Son and the Holy Spirit" or that immediately following Communion the Priest calls God to "save His people and bless His inheritance" or that the last audible prayer of the Liturgy prays that God "preserve the fullness of His Church." You go to the Liturgy to confess that you are a member of the Church of Christ.

3) *Sharing in the Symbolism.* The Divine Liturgy is symbolic also. It is common to see the Divine Liturgy as a symbolic re-enactment of the Life of Christ. The famous commentary of Nicholas Cabasilas on the Divine Liturgy is a classic treatment of the Divine Liturgy in this manner. Speaking, for instance, of the Prothesis he says:

> As long as the bread remains in the prothesis the portion thus separated from the rest is only bread. But it has acquired a new characteristic, it is dedicated to God; it has become an offering, since it represents our Lord during the first phase of his life on earth, when he became an oblation.

Nor is this a late development only. In the early Church St. Cyprian wrote of the Bread, Wine, and Water as symbols of the Unity of the Church.

... The Lord's sacrifices themselves declare that

54

Christian unanimity is linked together with itself by a firm and inseparable charity. For when the Lord calls bread, which is combined by the union of many grains, His body, He indicates our people whom He bore as being united; and when He calls the wine, which is pressed from many grapes and clusters and collected together, His blood, He also signifies our flock linked together by the mingling of a united multitude.

Today the Divine Liturgy is often seen as a divine drama, a kind of "passion play" of the Life of Christ. This symbolism can be outlined in the following manner:

The Prothesis represents the birth of Christ, hidden away from general notice, during which the Bread and Wine are prepared.

The Little Entrance with the Gospel reminds us of the beginning of Christ's public ministry and the first reason why the Lord came into the world, which was to teach humanity the Truth of God.

The Scripture Readings and the Sermon symbolize Christ, who through the readers of the Epistle and the Gospel and the preacher, teaches us His great truths.

The Great Entrance with the Holy Gifts stands for the second reason why Christ came into the world: that is, to die for us upon the Cross. This is indicated by the repetition of the words of the penitent thief, slightly modified: "Remember us all when thou comest into thy Kingdom . . ." during the Great Entrance.

The Words of the Institution of the Sacrament are a reminder of the Last Supper.

The Consecration of the Gifts is our presence at the Crucifixion when Jesus offered His Body and Blood for all mankind upon the Cross.

The Holy Communion is our sharing in the new life of the Resurrected Lord. The coming forth of the chalice from the Royal Gates parallels the coming forth of the Risen Lord from the tomb.

The Return of the Gifts to the Prothesis symbolizes the Ascension of our Lord and His return to the right hand of the Father.

Further, the Church Building itself, with its traditional architecture is often seen as a symbol of the whole universe, from a Christian perspective. It provides the setting for the drama of the liturgical re-enactment of the life of Christ. The German historian Oswald Spengler noted a fundamental distinction between the architecture of the temples of ancient Greece (upon which Byzantine Church architecture is based) and that of western, Gothic tradition.

The Gothic Church and all the styles dependent upon it, such as the New England Colonial Churches with their single spire, give the impression of upward seeking and movement. Man stands with his feet firmly planted on the earth, the architecture says, and he stretches his hands upward, searching after God, straining every spiritual nerve and muscle to the very tips of his fingers, seeking to reach Him. Gothic architecture with its multitude of upreaching spires symbolizes western man's active searching for God.

Spengler, however, noted that the Greek temple was quite different. It is complete in itself; it is not "going anywhere" and it is "not struggling" for anything. It has found its completion, its balance. This is also true of the Byzantine Church. Compare its domes with the spires of the Gothic tradition. Commentators addicted to symbolism see the whole universe—understood theologically—as included within the floor, ceiling, and four walls of the Church building. The dome is heaven; the floor, the earth; the narthex represents the non-believers (it was there when the Catechumens attended the Divine Liturgy); the nave, where the worshippers now stand represents the faithful Christians. This static, inclusive and "geographic" symbolism, however, becomes dynamic and active when the symbolism of the eastern or altar portion of the Church is considered. The Apse, which nearly always holds the icon of the Mother of God holding the Christ Child, is a symbol of the most important way by which "heaven" (the dome) and "earth" (the Christians) are joined together. The icon of the mother of God, and of the Christ child, oftentimes referred to as the "Platytera" is in reality an icon of the Incarnation. It dramatically and dynamically joins—architecturally—the dome and the area where the faithful stay. Symbolically, it points to the great Christian truth that one of the most important ways by which God is joined to man, and *vice versa* is through the Incarnation of the Son of God.

The remaining articles of furniture in the Altar area of the Church may also be seen symbolically: the Cantor's lectern and the Choir stalls represent our Godward prayers and praise; the Bishop's throne with its traditional icon of Christ, the High-Priest; the Pulpit, with its obvious symbolism of the Word of God; and most impressively, the Iconostasis, with its rows of icons.

The icons of the Iconostasis obviously point to those persons, groups, and events which dynamically show the relationship between God and man. The icons of Christ and the Theotokos are obvious. The Saints' icons, the recently traditional icon of the Last Supper over the Royal Gate, and other icons display the ways and the people through whom God and man have been united. All these point to what the theologians and philosophers call the "immanence" of God; that is, His presence and activity among us. However, the Iconostasis points to the opposite truth, also. The Iconostasis is a barrier; it separates the faithful from the "Holy of Holies," thereby symbolizing the truth that God is God, and man is man; that God is the Creator and that man is the creature. God is both with us, and distinct from us. God is both "immanent" and "transcendent."

Church buildings are symbolic structures. Those persons who study the history of church buildings frequently point to the fact that the architecture of the church is made to conform, in time, to the religious ideas of those who worship there. One of them has written this very interesting paragraph, which supports what has been said above.

> The church building not only commemorates the great moments of our Lord's life, but also the places in which these events took place ... So the church building which carries within it the summing up of that short period, not only commemorates the events of our Lord's life but in the act of commemoration actually re-enacts all the Gos-

pel scenes which took place in those days around Jerusalem. In some way, therefore, the church must not just represent but, through Eucharistic action, be identical with the upper room of the Last Supper as well as the two mountains of the anamesis: Calvary and Olivet.

Why have we spent so much time pointing to the symbolic dimension of the Divine Liturgy? Because today there is the movement among many scholars who study the Divine Liturgy to downplay and ignore the symbolic dimension of the Liturgy. There is danger in this. From the perspective of participation in the Divine Liturgy, there are many times when the symbolism can be of great assistance to the worshipper in his or her worship experience. It would be not proper to discount centuries of Orthodox Christian Liturgical piety by rigidly casting out all reference to symbolism as we learn to participate in the Divine Liturgy.

Yet, it is also true that Symbolism can be overdone. Many commentators get so involved in "interpreting" all the details, that the main sacramental, eucharistic, and sacrificial character of the Divine Liturgy is lost in a welter of disjointed and artificial symbolisms. In many cases, to use the words of one scholar, "one can see in general how far-fetched, fanciful, and unfounded some of these symbolic interpretations of the rites of the Divine Liturgy are, and how unrelated they are to the ceremonies and functions themselves." Yet, the same author, who is highly critical of the symbolic approach admits what—for us in this book—is the crucial point:

> The mystagogues of the past centuries were primarily interested in the subjective-ascetic aspect of interpretation; hence, they endowed every rite with a mystical meaning, in order to impress the reader and incite him to meditate upon the events of the redemption. Such interpretations undoubtedly were edifying and increased devotion, but at the same time they caused the historic practical aspect of the rites of the Divine Liturgy to be neglected.

The point of all of this is to indicate that symbolism has a place in encouraging participation by the Christian in the Divine Liturgy. It is not the only way of looking at and participating in the Divine Liturgy. But because the symbolic approach can "impress" the Christian" and incite him to meditate upon the events of the redemption," it is "edifying and increas(es) devotion." Seeing the symbolic meaning of the Divine Liturgy is one of several ways of participating in the Divine Liturgy. If you are going to genuinely participate in the Divine Liturgy, you will take into account its symbolic dimensions.

You do this by first knowing the symbolic meaning of the liturgical act in which you share. But that isn't enough. You must place yourself with your thoughts and feelings "in" the event. You should use your imagination to make yourself present at the event symbolized. For instance, when the Little Entrance takes place, symbolizing the fact that Jesus Christ has come into the world to teach us His great truths, use your imagination, your thoughts and feelings to experience this. What would you feel, what thoughts would come to your mind, what mood would you be in if you saw your Lord, walking toward the place where He would teach? What would you feel in your heart if, during the Great Entrance, you recognized Christ bearing His Cross on the way to Golgotha to be crucified? What prayers would rise to your mind if you imagined yourself in a darkened corner of the Upper Room as you hear Jesus saying, "This is my body . . . this is my blood"?

One of the best ways to participate in the Liturgy is to immerse yourself in its symbolism with your mind and heart and imagination.

4) *Responding to Dialogues and Biddings.* Another element in the Divine Liturgy which helps the Orthodox Christian participate in the Divine Liturgy are the "bidings" and the "dialogues" which make up a substantial part of the Service. Oftentimes we don't recognize that the very words of the Divine Liturgy call out for our participation. In fact, certain portions of the Divine Liturgy really don't make any sense without the active participation of the lay people. Here are a few

examples. Several times during the Divine Liturgy there are "litanies," which consist of a series of petitions said by the Priest. In these petitions the Priest asks the people to pray for specific things; he does not pray for them himself, and the choir merely responds "Lord have mercy." At the beginning of the Divine Liturgy, for instance, there is a litany in which the Priest says:

> For the peace of the whole world, for the stability of the Holy Churches of God, and for the union of all, let us pray to the Lord.

Notice what is happening. The Priest is not praying to God. He is directing himself to all the people gathered in the Church. He is asking *them* to pray for world peace, for the well-being and prosperity of the Church and for unity. The choir, in responding "Lord have mercy" to this and all the petitions, is not specifically responding to what the Priest is directing the congregation to do. And the people at best are merely "following the Service." The fact is that no one is actually praying for world peace, for the Church, or for "the union of all"!

What should be happening is obvious. The people should be praying for these things. You as a member of the laity should be exercising your "Spiritual Priesthood" during the Litany by offering your personal prayer for the things which the Priest is suggesting in each of the "biddings" of the Litany. For example, you could say in response to the petition referred to above:

> O Lord, grant peace to the peoples everywhere on the earth who are involved in armed conflict. Bring peace to all nations. Help the Church and its message to reach all of mankind.

Each time you hear that petition you can respond to it differently, emphasizing one or the other aspect. You should feel free to respond to the biddings in accordance to your own concerns as they have appeared throughout the preceding week. For instance, personal issues regarding non-Orthodox friends and aquaintances could be commended to God at the petition mentioned above. Prayerful support for negotiations begun to end military strife anywhere in the world could also be expressed.

Your response to each of the petitions of the Litanies should be brief, thoughtful and made with feeling. As you become accustomed to doing this, you will learn to anticipate what the Priest is saying and you may even have time to join the choir in singing the "Lord have mercy."

Similarly, there are several "dialogues" in the Divine Liturgy, where the Priest speaks directly to the people and the people respond to him. It is amazing to see what happens during these dialogues in so many of our Churches. Nothing! The Priest says, for instance, "Peace be unto all." The congregation shows no sign that it has received a blessing. Nor does the Priest, often, when the choir returns the blessing on behalf of the people: "And with thy spirit." These words are spoken by Priest to people and by the people to the Priest. They should not be mindless sounds uttered into a void. You should make these words your own words. You should say them with meaning and you should receive them as personally directed to you and all your fellow Christians. Some of these dialogues are listed below. As you read them say them as they are meant to be said: as a conversation between you and your Priest.

Before the Gospel:
>Priest: Wisdom! Attend! Let us hear the Holy Gospel.
>Peace unto all.
>People: And to thy spirit.

Before the Creed:
>Priest: Peace unto all.
>People: And with thy spirit.
>Priest: Let us love one another, that we may with one mind confess:
>People: The Father, Son and Holy Spirit. Trinity one in substance and undivided.

Before the Great Eucharistic Prayer:
>Priest: The grace of our Lord Jesus Christ, and the Love of God the Father, and the communion of the Holy Spirit be with you all.
>People: And with thy spirit.
>Priest: Let us lift up our hearts.
>People: We lift them up to the Lord.
>Priest: Let us give thanks unto the Lord.
>People: It is meet and right.

61

Participation in the Divine Liturgy means sharing actively in these parts of the Service which specifically call for your response. Praying for the things which the Priest suggests in the Litanies and consciously sharing in the dialogues will make your presence at the Divine Liturgy a more meaningful experience for you.

5) *Singing the Hymns.* At one time, in the history of the Church's worship there were no choirs. The people sang all of the hymns. Now there are choirs in every Church; and in a majority of our Orthodox Churches, the people never sing! What an unfortunate turnabout! No one advocates the abolishment of our choirs, but the restoration of congregational singing in one form or another is a real requirement, if the Orthodox laity is ever to become involved in the Liturgy in more than a spectator fashion. For unless we do this, we will continue to violate the spirit of both the Scripture and the Tradition of our Holy Orthodox Church. Jesus' Disciples are recorded as singing hymns with Him at the Last Supper. In the early Church, Christians were instructed in the following manner: ". . . assemble yourselves together every day, morning and evening, singing psalms and praying in the Lord's house . . . and on the day of our Lord's Resurrection, which is the Lord's Day, meet more diligently, sending praise to God."

Given the fact that choirs do make up an important part of our present day Church worship, in practice, how shall the laity join in the singing? First, it should be clear that there are some hymns which will probably always be reserved for the choirs. The Cherubic Hymn and the "It is meet to magnify thee on Theotokos" (Axion Estin) and "Holy, Holy, Holy" are anthems of sufficient complexity that will always demand the expert training and direction of a choir.

But there are numerous other hymns which are easily learned and sung. Several hymns, for instance, are both short and repeated. Among these are:

"Through the intercession of the Theotokos, Savior, save us." (First Antiphon)
"O Son of God who didst rise from the dead, save us

who sing to Thee; Alleluia." (Second Antiphon)
"Holy God, Holy Mighty, Holy Immortal, have mercy
on us."
"Glory to Thee, O Lord, Glory to Thee"
"Blessed be the Name of the Lord, from this time forth
and forever more."

Such hymns can easily be taught to the people by
the Priest with the cooperation of the choir director. Some
Priests have used the sermon over a period of Sundays
to teach the people the meaning and tradition of hymn-
singing in the Orthodox Church and then followed this
with a "sermon" instructing the people in singing the
hymns themselves. In most parishes this can be done
easily and effectively in just a few weeks. Certainly,
Priests will find it well worth the effort when they see
the interest and response of the faithful as they restore
the ancient practice of congregational singing to the
Church. Of course, some of our Orthodox jurisdictions
never lost this practice and retain it to this very day.
We will all agree that they are an example for the rest
of us.

However, even if congregational singing is still not
practiced in your parish church, you still may participate
in the singing of the hymns. There is an ancient and
venerable tradition of the Orthodox Church called "hypo-
psallein" which means to "subsing." Subsinging is the
practice of softly singing along with the choir or cantor.
As the hymn is being sung aloud by the Choir, you may
join in the singing. Do not sing so loud that you disturb
your neighbor, or permit discordance. But neither should
you let anyone prohibit you from subsinging the hymns
of the Divine Liturgy. It is both a right granted to you
by Tradition and responsibility of the worshipping Christian to join in the singing of hymns .

One final point must be made regarding hymn-singing.
Once we get into the practice of singing hymns, we meet
another danger that many choir members often notice.
We can get caught up in the rhythms and music of the
hymns and fail to realize that the words of the hymns
should become our own words of prayer. In the face of

that temptation we will agree with St. Paul who said, "What am I to do? I will pray with the spirit and I will pray with the mind also: I will sing with the spirit and I will sing with the mind also."

Our participation in the Divine Liturgy is enhanced when we sing or subsing the hymns of the Service with consciousness of the words we are saying, and making the words of the hymns our own, as expressions of our own love and faith in God.

6) *Reciting the Creed and the Lord's Prayer.* There are only two portions of the Divine Liturgy which are recited. The rest of the Service is usually chanted or sung. The two parts which are recited are in the central section of the Liturgy—one preceding the Great Eucharistic prayer, and the other following it. The Creed is the first; it is followed by the Lord's Prayer. In many Churches it is the practice to have the chantor, or an altar boy or the choir repeat these two recitative parts of the Divine Liturgy. Needless to say, this is not the best way. It is very much in the spirit of both the Creed and the Lord's Prayer that they be said by all the people in attendance; clergy, choir, and worshippers.

The Creed presently is written in the singular—"I believe in one God . . ." However, in the original form, it is in the plural—"We believe in one God . . ." for it was formed by an Ecumenical Council to express the faith of all Christians. The change to the singular is understandable for use in private worship, but its use in the plural for public worship is probably more correct. The Lord's Prayer was given by Christ to His disciples at their request for instructions as to how to pray. "Teach *us* to pray, Lord," they asked. "In this manner shall *ye* pray," the Lord responded, "*Our* Father who art in heaven . . . Give *us* this day *our* daily bread and forgive *us our* trespasses as *we* forgive those who trespass against *us*. And lead *us* not into temptation, but deliver *us* from evil."

It is clear that the recitations of the Divine Liturgy are designed to be said by all the people and not by just a single person or a representative group. Pastors should encourage all the people to recite both the Creed and the Lord's Prayer during the Divine Liturgy.

Recitation of the Creed and the Lord's Prayer, however, does not need to wait the introduction of a corporate system in those parishes where the practice is still to have the chantor, altar boy or choir saying them. Just as the worshipper can "subsing" the hymns, so he can quietly recite these portions to himself while they are being said aloud.

More important is the necessity that we make the words of the Creed and the Lord's Prayer real expressions of our Faith and belief. We must recite them conscientiously, thoughtfully, and with feeling. It does little good to have the words on your lips and the meaning of the words absent from your heart and mind. The prophet Isaiah records God accusing the ancient Israelites of the same fault, when he wrote "the people praise me with the tongue but their heart is far from me . . ."

When the Creed and the Lord's Prayer are repeated in the Liturgy you should make a special effort to recite the words with full consciousness of their meaning. This is more difficult to do with the Creed than with the Lord's Prayer, because the Lord's Prayer is both shorter and obviously a prayer. The Creed, however, can be equally meaningful to you. One way to help this to happen is to ask yourself, "To whom am I saying the Creed?" Rather than saying it as a proclamation to no one in particular, learn to direct your words to God Himself! The Creed takes on a totally new perspective when you consciously say it as a prayer to God, rather than as a statement in the air!

7) *Using Your Body to Worship.* The Divine Liturgy calls us to use our bodies in worship also, both figuratively and actually. "Let us raise our hearts unto the Lord," the Priest says to the people in a figurative way. But he also speaks quite literally when he says, "Let us bow our heads unto the Lord." The use of bodily movements and positions during the Divine Liturgy is an important method of participation. We should not think that it is necessary to stand at rigid attention, immobile and unbending in order to show proper respect. Unfortunately

for many of us, this unhappy instruction was the only guidance we ever received from our parents for attending Church Services: "Don't move!" "Stand straight!" Such injunctions may be appropriate for fidgety children, but they are not really appropriate for the Orthodox Christian worshipper.

In fact, the traditional absence of pews in Orthodox Churches was designed to permit movement and activity during the Divine Liturgy. The people would reverence icons, kneel, make repeated genuflections (metanoies), and bow frequently during the Service in a free and uninhibited manner in traditional Orthodox worship. They worshipped with their bodies as well as with their souls!

How different it is in many Orthodox parishes today! We have adopted a severe "school house" attitude where Christians remain ramrod-straight, unbending and rigidly formal. Yet the liturgical practice of the Service calls upon us to respond in worship with our bodies! At the Little Entrance, the Priest dramatically calls us to "worship and fall down before Christ"; the least we should do, in response, is to bow from the waist, making the sign of the Cross. Many times during the Divine Liturgy the Priest blesses the people saying "Peace be to all." Certainly it is appropriate to bow your head to receive the blessing. No less appropriate is the same response by the Priest when the people return the blessing with the words, "and to thy spirit." Certainly, the same response is fitting during the Great Entrance when the Priest passes before us carrying the Holy Gifts and representing the Lord bearing His Cross. The same holds true when the Priest censes the Church and the people. Should you not bow your head, remembering that the incense is a symbol representing your prayers as they rise Godward? Elsewhere, we are called to attention, when just before the most holy portion of the Divine Liturgy—the Great Eucharistic Prayer—the Priest calls, "Let us stand aright; let us stand with fear; let us attend, that we may make the Holy Offering in peace." Even our leaving has significance—"Let us go forth in peace," we are instructed.

However, the most important bodily movement in worship by the Orthodox Christian is the "sign of the Cross." Here too, the need is to make the sign of the Cross something more than an automatic response, indulged in without thought or feeling. What is it that we do when we Orthodox Christians make the sign of the Cross? Many things: we identify ourselves as Orthodox Christians; we confess our faith in the Holy Trinity; we express devotion; we bless ourselves. Christians, like St. Paul, "glory in the Cross." But to do so requires that we make the "sign of the Cross" with care. Sometimes it seems that many of the faithful are not making the sign of the Cross at all, but rather, "the sign of the banjo," or "the sign of the arc" or "the sign of the circle"! It is much better to make the sign of the Cross less frequently and with more deliberation, devotion, and feeling than to do it many times without care. The sign of the Cross should be your outward expression of an attitude of worship and devotion.

8) *Listening to the Readings and Sermon.* It may appear unnecessary to you to make the following comments, but experience proves the contrary. The Divine Liturgy has three portions where the people are directly instructed: the Epistle reading, the Gospel reading; and the Sermon.

In these acts, God instructs us—through the reader, the Priest and the Preacher—of the Divine Truths which are so needed to enlighten our minds toward Christian living. Yet, for many, the readings and the Sermon are occasions for our minds to wander. There is a dimension to participation in the Divine Liturgy which is simply attentiveness. When the Epistle and Gospel are read, we should strain our inner ear to understand the message. Many parishes provide their members with a Church calendar which lists the Scripture readings for each Sunday. Wouldn't you profit a great deal if you made it a habit to read these passages from your own Bible Saturday night or Sunday morning before going to Church? If someone is speaking to us in a conversation and we ignore him as he talks, it is an insult to him. Is that not what we do when we fail to give heed to the Scripture readings and the preaching of God's Word? An ancient writer of the Church challenges us about this aspect of our Sunday Church attendance: "What apology will that Christian make to God, who does not assemble on that day *to hear* the saving Word?"

9) *Using the "Units" of the Divine Liturgy.* In the previous Chapter we discussed the makeup and structure of the Divine Liturgy. We saw how the Divine Liturgy consists of nine sections, each of which has a purpose and dominant feature which give meaning to it.

Participating in the Divine Liturgy means keeping the meaning and purpose of each of the nine units of the Divine Liturgy before you as you worship. When, for example, you note that the fifth section of the Liturgy is dedicated to the Scripture readings, you are reminded what you are to be doing during this part of the Service. Keeping yourself aware of the structure and of the purpose of each "pearl" of the Divine Liturgy will help make the Divine Liturgy a more meaningful experience for you, since you will have a confident feeling that you not only "know what is going on," but that you are also helping it happen.

10) *"Praying the Divine Liturgy."* Perhaps the most inclusive way to describe how to participate in the Divine Liturgy is to "Pray the Liturgy." All of the methods of participation which we have described above require that we pray when we attend the Divine Liturgy. It would seem that it is hardly necessary to say this. Yet, many will agree that it is an instruction which must be made.

Years of pastoral experience have convinced many Priests that numerous Christians attend Church without ever uttering a single conscious prayer! There are many Christians who come to Church out of a sense of duty, or who attend expecting that the chanting, the music, the icons, the incense, and the whole atmosphere will *act* on them, while they passively receive them into their spirits.

Yet, as we have seen above, and as we shall see in more detail in the chapters to come, the whole Divine Liturgy, as an act of worship by the Priest and the people, presupposes an actively praying body of worshippers. In fact, the Divine Liturgy is nothing more than prayer, with only a few exceptions. Much of the Liturgy invites you to pray not only the formal prayers, but also to create your own prayers during the Service. You should bring your daily concerns with you to the Liturgy, and offer them up to God. For instance, when in the Litanies you are invited to pray for "travelers by sea, by land, and by air; for the sick and suffering; for captives and their salvation," you have a range of topics to pray for that is inexhaustible. In that one case alone, you may remember in prayer such diverse concerns as victims of auto, train, and airplane accidents, skyjackings; relatives, friends, and aquaintances who are ill or hospitalized; political prisoners, and even prison inmates. You should feel free to include your personal concerns in the prayers you offer the Divine Liturgy as you exercise your "Spiritual Priesthood."

Further, you may join the Priest as he reads the inaudible prayers. They are printed in all the Liturgy handbooks for your use. At one time in the Church's history they were said aloud for all to share. Now, with the singing of hymns by the choirs, the worshipping Christian has the time both to repeat the hymn with his own words and to read the prayer together with the Priest.

There are so many different ways for you to "Pray the Liturgy" that no Sunday ever has to be the same as any other. Each Divine Liturgy can have fresh, new and inspiring content for you. If you truly "Pray the Liturgy" you will never be bored, never feel unrefreshed, never lose the vitality, excitement and vigor of the Living Liturgy.

As you enter the Church, lighting your candle and reverencing the icons—pray! As you are called to participate in the Litanies—pray! As you join in the hymns—pray! As you think of the meaning of the symbolic acts—pray! As you read the inaudible parts—pray! As you recite the Creed—pray! As you approach the Chalice for Holy Communion—pray! Instruct yourself as you go to Church each Sunday to "Pray the Liturgy." Prayer, no matter how offered, is essential to participation in the Divine Liturgy.

You Have to Put Something Into It

We have seen in the preceding pages ten ways that lay people can participate in the Divine Liturgy. These ways are:

1) Receiving Holy Communion
2) Being the Church
3) Sharing in the Symbolism
4) Responding to Dialogues and Biddings
5) Singing the Hymns
6) Reciting the Creed and the Lord's Prayer
7) Using Your Body in Worship
8) Listening to the Readings and Sermon
9) Using the "Units" of the Divine Liturgy
10) "Praying the Liturgy"

As we have seen, the Divine Liturgy itself invites us to participate in these various ways; they are not imposed on the Service of the Divine Liturgy of St. John Chrysostom from the outside.

These ten ways are the natural and appropriate methods for the Orthodox Christian to share in the Liturgy. We have also seen that each time we worship we are free to use any or all of these methods as we participate, even at the same places. For instance, at the Cherubic Hymn and its Great Entrance, we can sing the hymn, pray the inaudible prayer with the Priest, immerse ourselves in the symbolism of the Great Entrance, find a topic to mediate upon, etc. No divine Liturgy has to be exactly the same as any other for us! Every Divine Liturgy can and should be a fresh, new, and inspiring worship experience. With the knowledge that you now have, your attendance at the Divine Liturgy can be meaningful, interesting, and enriching. You can "Get *much* out of the Liturgy."

Participation, however, takes more than knowledge. Participation takes some effort. It requires attentive activity. It requires deliberate interest and effort. In order to get something out of the Liturgy, you must put something into it. It has always been this way. In the fourth century book, *Constitutions of the Holy Apostles*, Christians are instructed that " . . . the trades of the faithful

70

are works of passing significance for your maintenance; but make the worship of God your main business."

Go to the Divine Liturgy each Sunday knowing that you go there to act. In the Liturgy you are not a passive recipient of religious influences. You are there to do something. You attend the Divine Liturgy to exercise your Spiritual Priesthood together with all the other Orthodox Faithful under the direction and leadership of your Sacerdotal Priest. You have a job to do! You have work to perform. It is spiritual work; work of the heart and work of the mind. You must enter heart, soul, and mind into the spirit of the words and acts of the Liturgy, making all of them your own. You must draw your resources together, concentrating your attention on the Liturgy and freeing yourself from distractions and disturbances. Many years ago, St. Isaac the Syrian gave the same kind of advice to those under his spiritual care when he said:

> Do you wish to enjoy the words of your services and to understand the meaning of the words of the Spirit that you utter? Then ... let your mind sink deep into study of the words of the Spirit, till your soul is roused to heights of understanding and thereby is moved to glorify God ... There is no peace for the mind in slavish work (in merely reading the set prayers); and disturbance of mind deprives it of the taste of the meaning and of understanding.

The rest of this book will take you word by word and step by step through the Divine Liturgy of St. John Chrysostom as it is today, giving you specific suggestions and methods for each of the sections of the Liturgy. You will be concretely, specifically, and practically shown how you can participate at each step of the Liturgy—not rigidly or in a formal manner, but freely and joyfully.

However, the emphasis is on you. *You* must act. *You* must participate. *You* must pray the Liturgy. Hopefully, with the specific guidance provided in the next two Chapters, you will learn to truly put "Life in the Liturgy."

CHAPTER FOUR

Life in the Liturgy (I)

We now turn our attention to the text of the Divine Liturgy with participation in mind. In accordance with what was previously said, we will expect to see the Divine Liturgy sectioned into nine distinct parts, each of which having its own purpose, is readily identifiable. These divisions thus help us set our mind and heart and spirit into a mood of active participation. All the sections are are part of the organic whole which is the Divine Liturgy itself. As Cabasilas says: "The whole celebration of the mystery is like the unique portrayal of a single body, which from beginning to end preserves its order and harmony, so that each ceremony, each prayer, adds something to the whole." As we proceed we will identify these nine sections concretely in the text of the Divine Liturgy. In most cases, as we have already pointed out, the sign that a section is ended is the Shorter Litany, which consists of a relatively standard repetition of the words, "Help, save, be merciful and protect us, O God, by thy grace," followed by "Lord have mercy" and "Commemorating our most Holy, pure, blessed and glorified Lady, the Mother of God and Ever-Virgin Mary, with all the Saints, let us commend ourselves and one another, and our whole life to Christ our God," with the response "To Thee O Lord." Then this is followed by an ascription to the Holy Trinity preceded by a phrase which constantly changes in specific content. Later when we look at the Shorter Litany more closely and from a perspective of specific participation we will note that this changing introductory part of ascription to the Trinity answers one of two questions which are assumed to be in the thoughts of the worshippers. In the case of the first section of the Liturgy, the ascription to the Trinity is: "For unto thee are due all glory, honor, and worship, to the Father, and to the Son, and to the Holy Spirit; now and ever and unto ages of ages," the choir responding "Amen."

This pattern of each section which is completed by the Shorter Litany with its changing ascription introduces us to another liturgical reality. The structure of sections in the Liturgy is not mechanically applied. As we proceed we will discover that the structural pattern of the present day Liturgy varies both in form and content. It is very much the same as in a symphony with its theme and the variations on the theme. However, in most cases the variation is quite readily evident to us, once we are aware of the basic pattern. All this will come clear as we begin to go over the Liturgy word by word and phrase by phrase.

The apprehension of the structure of the Divine Liturgy is the first step which begins our journey through the Divine Liturgy in a conscious, active, and spiritually rewarding manner. The second is the recognition of the specific ways of personal and active participation in the Divine Liturgy as it presently stands. In the preceding chapter we discussed these at some length. Let us then consciously bring together on the one hand, our understanding of the structure of the Divine Liturgy and on the other, the various ways we personally participate in the Divine Liturgy. Let us hold them together as we approach the Divine Drama of worship in the Orthodox Church with faith, reverence, and intent zeal. We now begin a phrase by phrase practical study of our effort to actively participate in the Liturgy.

The Beginning of the Divine Liturgy

The Divine Liturgy begins with the words "Blessed is the Kingdom of the Father, of the Son, and of the Holy Spirit; now and ever, and unto ages of ages." Only two other Services begin with these words in our Liturgical Tradition; the Sacrament of Baptism and Holy Matrimony. As we have pointed out before, the Divine Liturgy is the Church being itself; that is, being the Kingdom of God. It is our glorious and wonderful privilege in consequence of the acts of God to be members of His Kingdom here and now and, we trust, in the future to come. For this we rejoice. We can readily begin our participation in the Divine Liturgy by repeating within ourselves the very words the Priest is saying with a feeling of conscious affirmation. We might also express this feeling with a silently offered prayer in which for example, we might pray, "Yes, truly blessed, O Holy Trinity, is thy Kingdom among us. Be with all the members of Thy Kingdom who have gathered together in this Temple." Such a short prayer, silently said in our own words and based on the subject of the liturgical prayer is one of the key methods of participation in the Divine Liturgy. The very words and the raised Gospel, the sign of the Cross, call upon us to make the sign of the Cross concurrently blessing ourselves with our prayer. The Liturgy has begun with this introductory blessing.

Part One: The Litany

The first of the nine sections of the Liturgy, the Litany, follows. This Litany begins with a call to prayer addressed by the Priest to the gathered congregation. "In Peace let us pray to the Lord." While most commentators mention the obvious fact that the people are being called to pray here, they never move to the next obvious step of encouraging people *to pray!* Cabasilas notes that we need guidance in what to pray for, quoting St. Paul who says "we know not what we should pray for as we ought." He continues:

> ... the Priest exhorts the people to prayer, for he is appointed to this office and is for this reason placed in front of the people ... those for whom he makes supplication contribute all they can, by their good behaviour, prayers, gentleness, and justice, and anything else which they know is pleasing to God.

And Demetrios Panagiotopoulos says that the Priest, with this phrase, "In Peace, let us pray to the Lord," urges

the faithful to pray and call on God with peace...."
A little further on he says, "All ought to be completely
given over to God and with a peaceful and calm spirit
ought to participate in the common prayer." Yet neither
he nor Cabasilas nor any other commentator then proceeds to make the obvious requirement of the worshipper to actually, consciously, and explicitly pray for
those things which he is called upon to pray for!

Let us see exactly what is meant by this. The first
specific call to prayer by the Priest is put in these words:

> For the Peace from above and for the salvation of our
> souls, let us pray to the Lord.

You are being called upon to pray for something quite
specific: "the peace from above" and "the salvation
of souls." The words are directed by the Priest to the
worshipper, not to God. So it is evident that the Priest
is not praying for these two things. What of the choir?
They are responding to the Priest's instructions with
the prayer, "Lord, have mercy," which serves to separate
the petitions, but in all honesty, is not a real response
to the Priest's specific call to pray for peace and salvation.
So the choir isn't praying for these things, either. The
only persons left in the Church who could possibly respond
to this specific request are the laity. If *they* do not pray
for the two specific topics in this call to prayer in the
Great Litany, then we face a rather embarrassing and
futile liturgical excercise. No one is praying for those
things! If the Priest is not praying, but directing the
laity to pray, and if the choir is not praying for those
things, and if you the worshippers are passively listening,
but nor responding to the Priest's request for you to
pray, NOTHING IS BEING DONE! We have the form
of worship and prayer, but no content. Such an obvious
state of affairs has never been commented upon! The
solution is equally self-evident. If the Priest is asking
you to pray for the "peace that comes from above" and
the "salvation of your souls," then, *pray for them!*

While the choir is singing the "Lord have mercy,"
you have time to mentally pray for these things. You
can do this in several ways. You can turn the words

of the Priest's instructions around into a prayer directed to God. Thus, you could respond by saying in mental prayer, "O God, grant us all peace from above and the salvation of our souls." You could also use only one of the terms as a theme for a brief prayer: "O Lord, grant thy peace to all of us gathered here, so that we may worship and glorify Thee without distraction." Or you may apply the petition to a specific situation or person whom you have in mind. In the case of this petition you might offer the prayer for your own salvation: "O God, sinner and unworthy though I be, look down upon me and in Thy mercy and save me." When we pray in any of these ways we are responding to the Priest's call to prayer. Then, the Litany not only takes on dynamic meaning and practical application, but it has also immediately drawn us into active spiritual participation in the Divine Liturgy.

The next call to specific prayer in the Liturgy includes three concrete blessings we can ask for: world peace, Church stability, and the unity of Christians.

> For the peace of the whole world; for the stability of the Holy Churches of God, and for the union of all, let us pray to the Lord.

Thus we could respond with any number of prayers, perhaps varying our response each time we attend the Divine Liturgy. For example, "O God, grant that the hostilities that our nation is now engaged in may soon end, that Thy peace might reign among us." Or, "Heavenly King, keep Thy Church in peace and undisturbed by controversy and strife." Or, "O Christ, Lord of the Church, lead all Christians to unity in truth and in spirit."

In the same manner, each of the following petitions gives us one or more themes or topics for a brief, one-sentence prayer. In response to these specific calls for prayer we can thus pray for the Church building in which we pray, the worshippers joining us, our Bishop, Metropolitan or Archbishop, our Priest and Deacon, the clergy and people in general, the President and civil authorities of our nation, our defense forces, the city in which we live, all cities and countries, and the faithful Christians throughout the world. We are also called upon to pray for good weather, bountiful harvests, general peace; for travelers, the sick and suffering; for captives, and for ourselves that we do not fall into dangerous situations. The last petition of the Great Litany is now followed by what we have called the Shorter Litany. It is the sign that a section of the Liturgy is coming to an end. The tone of the Priest's part changes now. Instead of speaking to the Faithful he directs his words to God, imploring God's aid and action on our behalf. "Help us, save us, have mercy and protect us, O God, by thy Grace." Here, participation means consciously repeating this prayer, word for word with the Priest; he is pleading aloud for all of us, and we silently identify ourselves with his plea. The choir's "Lord have mercy" can be participated in by the worshipper by subsinging. The Shorter Litany continues as the Priest calls to remembrance or commemorates the Mother of God and the Saints who gave themselves over completely to God. They are our example of the reality of the Church's life. In imitation of them we are called to give ourselves over completely as individuals and as members, one of another, to Christ.

> Commemorating our most Holy, pure, blessed, and glorified Lady, Theotokos, and Ever-Virgin Mary, with all the Saints, let us commend ourselves and one another and our whole life to Christ our God.

This frequently repeated phrase is the Priest's call to you to dedicate and re-dedicate your whole existence to Christ. As the Priest calls you to this rededication, the choir responds with the words, "To Thee, O Lord." This is our act of dedication and rededication. You may articulate your conscious and willed response to the Priest's call for this dedication of yourself and your whole life with a brief prayer: "Yes, O Lord, I rededicate my whole life and commend all others to Thee, the Saviour of our souls." Or, you may signify your agreement and reaffirmation of your devotion by bowing your head, making the sign of the Cross, subsinging with the choir either as individual acts of participation or simultaneously. The

77

important thing is that you consciously participate actively.

The Shorter Litany then concludes with an ascription to the Holy Trinity. Sometimes this ascription is in reality the ending of a prayer said inaudibly by the Priest, though it rarely is actually recited in that place. At other times the ascription appears to have no connection with any inaudible or audible liturgical prayer. In each case however, the ascription is preceded by a phrase which always varies but which also may be connected to the previous call to dedication of our whole lives to Christ with the assumed questions "Why?" or "How?" "*Why* should I commend my life to God; what are some of the things concerning God which invite my response of dedication and devotion?" Or, "*How* shall I devote myself to Him?" Thus Cabasilas writes: "(The Priest) concludes by giving the reason for his supplications . . ." These are not doubting questions, but the questions of a loving spirit counting the wonders of the Lord.

The first response to the implied question is: "For to thee are *due* all glory, and honor and worship." It is only proper that we dedicate ourselves to God; He is God, and that dedication is due Him. As the Priest says these words and repeats the names of the persons of the Holy Trinity, show your acknowledgement of the fact that such dedication is due Him by making the sign of the Cross and subsinging with the choir the words "Amen," which in Hebrew mean, "so be it" signifying your agreement and assent.

Thus the first section—a call to pray for specific things —comes to an end with the completion of the Shorter Litany. The first "pearl" of the Liturgy is put on the string. We have seen the intent and purpose of the first section of the Divine Liturgy and we have indicated the practical, positive, and specific ways in which we can participate. We now move to the second section.

Part Two: The First Antiphon

The next Section of the Liturgy is the First Antiphon.

In the shorter Liturgy described in the *Constitutions of the Holy Apostles* we have this instruction:

> ... when there have been two lessons (O.T.) severally read, let some other person sing the hymns of David, and *let the people join at the conclusions of the verses.* Afterwards let our acts be read, and the epistles of Paul our fellow-worker ... and afterwards let a deacon or presbyter read the Gospels.

In the commentary by Cabasilas, we read: "Then the Priest intones the sacred Psalms, and the chant is taken up by all present, who sing the inspired words of the holy prophets." Nikolai Gogol, reflecting the Russian tradition says, "The Antiphons are songs selected from the Psalms which prophetically represent the coming of the Son of God into the world, and are sung alternately by the two choirs on either side." This points to the meaning of the term "antiphon" from the Greek "anti" and "phone." From the *Synekdemos* prayerbook of the Ecumenical Patriarchate we see what the first of these psalms was: The 102 Psalm (in the Septuaguint, 103 in the King James Version) which begins with the words, "Bless the Lord, O My soul, and all that is within me, bless his holy name."

But in current liturgical practice in the Greek and other Churches this Psalm is not said. In its place a very short appeal to the Savior to save us through the intercessions of the Theotokos is sung three times. It appears that this was a refrain sung by the people *after* the reading of the psalm. The Psalm then dropped out of liturgical practice and the refrain remained. It appears that it was sung, even as a refrain, in an antiphonal manner. This means that an antiphon—to be an antiphon— must be sung at least twice.

How do we participate in this very short second section of the Liturgy? Obviously, if in your Church the 102nd Psalm is read or chanted, you may either listen carefully to this Scriptural passage, or, if it is chanted, you can sing along or subsing as the ancient author suggested. If, in your local parish, the 102nd Psalm is not sung, it is replaced by the Antiphon, "Through the intercessions of the Mother of God, O Saviour, save us." Again, you have several options regarding your mode of participation. You may subsing along with the choir, you may repeat the words quietly to yourself as an intimate prayer, or you may use the hymn as the theme of your own prayer: for example, "O Jesus Christ, thou who hast come into the world to save us, unworthy though we be, accept the prayers of thine own mother, the Holy Theotokos, on our behalf and redeem and cleanse us of our sins." Finally, we may readily participate in the Divine Liturgy in joining with the Priest as he inaudibly reads the "Prayer of the First Antiphon."

As soon as the First Antiphon has been sung for the third time, the Shorter Litany is again heard. "Again and again in peace let us Pray to the Lord" is the repeated call of the Priest. The worshippers join the choir in subsinging the "Lord have mercy" and we again join as described before in pleading with the Priest that God "Help, save, be merciful and protect us . . ." And again we respond to his call to "commend ourselves and one another and our whole life unto Christ our God," repeating the reaffirmation of our faith and dedication with the choir as we sing "To Thee, O Lord." Now another reason is presented as to why we should commend ourselves and one another to God. This time the reason given is God's Lordship over all of creation: "For Thine is the majesty and Thine is the Kingdom, and the power and the glory; of the Father and of the Son and of the Holy Spirit; now and ever, and unto ages of ages. Amen."

Thus, the second "pearl," the second section and unit of the Divine Liturgy, falls into place. It is the shortest and smallest of all, yet it lends its own meaning and beauty to the whole of the Service.

Part Three: The Second Antiphon

This portion of the Divine Liturgy is the second Antiphon. In the Russian Church and in the *Synekdemos* of the Church of Constantinople the 145th Psalm (Septuagint Version; 146th Psalm in the King James Version) is then read or chanted. It begins with the words, "Praise the Lord, O my soul! I will praise the Lord as long as I live; I will sing praises to my God while I have being . . ." In Churches where this beautiful liturgically and socially significant psalm is read or sung the worshipper participates by either listening attentively or by subsinging with the choir or chantor. However, in many Churches the 145th Psalm has been replaced by Antiphonal hymns. True to the principle "theme and variations" we have in the Second Antiphon, an antiphonal hymn with a difference: the antiphon—as it must be—is sung at least twice, depending on the liturgical text that you are using. For example, the *Synekdemos* calls for a fourfold repetition; that of the Antiochian versions, three times. The Antiphon itself is a beautiful appeal to the saving power of the Risen Lord. "O Son of God, Who didst rise from the dead, save us who sing unto Thee, Alleluia."

Participation in this portion of the Liturgy is much the same as that in the First Antiphon. Among your options for participation are subsinging, repetition of the words as a personal prayer, the use of the hymn as a theme for personally worded prayer, or you may join the Priest in praying the prayer of the Second Antiphon.

The variation in the theme and sequence is here seen in what follows. After a small Doxology the choir sings the hymn "O only begotten Son of God . . ." This ancient hymn is in fact a short creed, emphasizing in the form of liturgical poetry the two basic Christian beliefs and real experience of the Church: the Incarnation of Christ and the Doctrine of the Holy Trinity. Participation in this hymn can be either by subsinging or repeating the hymn as an affirmation of faith on your part as an individual and as a member of the Body of Christ, the Church. You express Faith through this hymn in Him "who didst deign, for our salvation to be incarnated through our most Holy Lady and Mother of God," who is "one of the Holy Trinity, and . . . glorified with the Father and the Holy Spirit."

We know that the third section of the Divine Liturgy is ending when we see that the Shorter Litany again is repeated. This time, another reason why we should commend ourselves and one another to God is presented: we ought to do so because our God has been good to us and loves us. "For thou art, O God, good and lovest mankind, and to Thee we ascribe glory; to the Father, and to the Son, and to the Holy Spirit; now and ever, and unto ages of ages. Amen."

Thus, with this variation of the now familiar pattern, the third "pearl," the third section of the Divine Liturgy, consisting of the Second Antiphon, falls into place.

Part Four: The Third Antiphon and Little Entrance

There is a Third Antiphon which is the fourth section of the Divine Liturgy. Regarding the Third Antiphon Panagiotopoulos explains:

> According to the Typicon (book of rubrics) on Sundays and regular feast days the beatitudes from the Gospel of Matthew (Matthew 5:3-12) are sung as the Third Antiphon, to which are added certain hymns from the Octoechos or the Canon of the Feast Day . . . For the sake of saving time it is customary to sing in the place of the Beatitudes the Dismissal Hymn of the tone of the day, that is, the last hymn of the Vespers which is followed by the dismissal. Also, on important Holy Days the Dismissal Hymn for the Feast is sung in the Third Antiphon.

Most Liturgy Handbooks include a supplement at the end of the Divine Liturgy itself in which the eight Dismissal Hymns of the Resurrection are listed. There are eight Dismissal Hymns of the Ressurection, one for each of the Eight Tones of Byzantine Ecclesiastical music. The Dismissal Hymn of the tone of the day is sung for the first time by the Priest, choir, or chantor. If you have the text before you, you can subsing, pray the text, or use its content as a theme for your own prayer.

However, again in the spirit of theme and variations something new now happens in the Liturgy. While the Third Antiphon is being sung for the first time, the Priest takes the Gospel Book from off the Altar Table, goes around the Holy Table, and preceded by the Acolytes bearing candles, he leaves the Altar area through the North door of the Iconostasis and enters the Nave or main portion of the Church. This is known as the Little Entrance and it takes place during the Third Antiphon. As we have seen before, the Little Entrance in the view of the Divine Liturgy as a reenactment of the Life of Christ, symbolizes the first reason why Jesus Christ came into the world. He came into the world and among men to teach. The Priest bears the golden Gospel Book preceded by the lighted tapers as he enters into the area of the Church building which represents that portion of the world which is receptive to Christ's Gospel Message. When the Third Antiphon is finished, the Priest, now in the center of the Church, raises up the Gospel Book and intones aloud "Wisdom! Let us arise."

How do we participate? Gogol, in his meditations gives us the clue. He writes:

> The Faithful look upon the Gospel which is carried in the hands of the humble ministers of the Church, as if it were the Saviour Himself going out for the first time to the work of Divine Preaching.

In a mystically symbolic way you are transported through time and space to the Holy Land. In your mind's eye and with reverent heart, you no longer see Priest and acolytes; it is Christ and His Disciples. Liturgically Christ comes toward you with the purpose of teaching the eternal verities of His Gospel to you and your fellow worshippers! What do you feel? What emotions well up in your heart? The Priest expresses your sense of awe and unworthiness as you stand before your Master and Lord! All the worshippers sing along with the Priest, bowing their heads and reverencing themselves in awesome respect as they find themselves in the presence of our Lord.

> Come, let us worship and bow unto Chirst. O Son of God, who didst rise from the dead; save us who sing unto Thee, Alleluia.

The best way of participating at this point of the Divine Liturgy is to imaginatively place yourself in the time and place where Christ approaches a group of people with the intent of teaching. Your heart and mind should become attentive and open. The Lord is about to begin His teaching!

When the Priest returns to the Altar Table with the Gospel Book, the choir or cantors repeat the Dismissal Hymn of the Resurrection for the day and it thus becomes an Antiphon, sung twice. Usually this is followed by a series of other Dismissal Hymns for the Saint of the day, the Dismissal Hymn of the patron Saint of that particular Church as well as certain other Troparia and Kontakia. Some liturgical handbooks have many of these listed in the Appendix. They are excerpts from the various liturgical books such as the *Menaia, Triodion,* and *Pentecostarion.* If the handbook that you are using has them, read them or subsing as the choir sings them. If not, you may listen attentively to the choir or contemplate your need for the wisdom of the Gospel of Christ. Of course, you may also pray the prayer of the Third Antiphon which the Priest reads during the first singing of the Dismissal Hymn if you have not done it before. Thus, again, we have many possible ways of participation. The Fourth Section of the Liturgy comes to an end with an abbreviated form of the Shorter Litany, "Let us entreat the Lord," the Priest says. The phrases "Help us, save us . . ." and "calling to remembrance" are not said. The Priest goes directly to the final ascription, which from its form must have been at one time preceded by the usual call to "commend ourselves and one another and our whole life to Christ our God," because the ascription begins with the justifying phrase "For Thou . . ." just as do all the preceding ascriptions. We assume that we are again being given another reason why we should commend ourselves and one another to Christ:

> For Thou our God are Holy, and to Thee we ascribe glory; to the Father, and to the Son, and to the Holy Spirit, now and forever, and unto ages of ages. Amen.

With this, the fourth "pearl"—a beautiful section, full of dramatic symbolism—is ended. We have experienced the first reason why Christ, the Son of God, became Man; to teach us. Now, as we move to the next section we will hear that teaching.

Part Five: The Scripture Readings

The Fifth Section of the Divine Liturgy consists of the content of the message of Christ. In the previous section we saw Christ come to us in order to teach. In this section, through the Epistle and Gospel readings, and the Sermon, Christ speaks to us and His message is made alive for us.

This unit of the Liturgy of St. John Chrysostom begins with the famous Orthodox "Trisagion Prayer." Practically every Service in the Typicon of the Orthodox Church includes this Trisagion Prayer. If we look at it carefully we will see that the first and greater part of this prayer is an awesome call upon the name of God. Just as the words "Our Father" form the address of the Lord's Prayer, here the words, "Holy God, Holy Mighty One, Holy Immortal" are not informative statements about God, but rather expressions of the awed reverence of a sinful creature as he stands before the Completely Other, The Transcendent, the All-powerful and Eternal Being whom he calls God. "Holy God" we whisper in awe and reverence; "Holy Mighty One" we address Him, fully cognizant of our own weakness; "Holy Immortal," we mortal time-bound beings name the Everlasting One. And then humbly, with His greatness and our smallness evident before us, we petition, "Have Mercy on us!"

In the Divine Liturgy the choir sings the Trisagion prayer. You can participate by subsinging, by contemplating its meaning, by bowing your head and making the sign of the Cross submissively. Or you may participate by reading the beautiful prayer which the Priest says inaudibly in which these words are uttered: "Do Thou, O Lord, accept even from the mouths of us sinners the Trisagion Hymn, and graciously look down upon us."

When the Trisagion hymn is over, putting us in the proper spirit for the reception of the Word of God, the Epistle and Gospel are read. The Priest calls you to attend to the reading in both cases, and calls our attention to the fact that we are about to hear Divine Wisdom: "Wisdom, let us attend!" he says before the Epistle Reading. When the appointed reading has been completed by the Reader, the Priest blesses him saying, "Peace be to thee that readest." The people and choir respond three times with the Hebrew word for "Glory to Thee O God," "Alleluia, Alleluia, Alleluia."

During this reading, the Priest recites an inaudible prayer requesting illumination of heart and mind for the full understanding of the Gospel of Christ. The Priest then announces the Gospel "Wisdom! Attend! Let us hear the Holy Gospel." In preparation so that they may properly receive the Gospel's message, the Priest blesses the people, "Peace be to all." The worshippers enter into a dialogue with the Priest.

You should participate by consciously receiving the Priest's blessing and bowing your head. Then you should share in the dialogue by returning the blessing, saying with the choir, "And with thy spirit." Of course, the most important manner of participation is to listen to the readings with real attention and care. You may also choose to read the "Prayer before the Gospel," together with the Priest as a way of preparing yourself for the Scripture Readings, as noted above. A good practice to get into is reading the appointed Epistle and Gospel passages before coming to Church. Both will mean more to you as you listen to them chanted or read in the Service.

This is the correct and proper place for the Sermon. In some parishes, the Priest, however, chooses to preach at the end of the Divine Liturgy for practical reasons. Regardless of the practice in your parish, when the Sermon is preached, you should put yourself in a receptive, attentive attitude. The preacher is an instrument of God's Word, interpreting the Scriptures which, according to St. Paul, are "profitable for doctrine, for reproof, for correction, for instruction in righteousness: that the man of God may be perfect, thoroughly furnished unto all good works." The Sermon is preached to help you become a better Christian, to instruct and enlighten you. Open your heart and mind to hear that word of instruction with the resolve to put into practice what you hear.

The reading of the Scriptures is then followed by a longer Litany referred to as the "Ektenia of Fervent Supplication" coupled with the readings of the prayers for the Catechumens and for the Faithful. Here the different jurisdictions of the Orthodox Church in the Americas vary their practices greatly. Some of the jurisdictions say the whole Ektenia and all the prayers. Others say some of the Ektenia and some of the prayers. At least one of the jurisdictions says none of them. If in your parish, the Ektenia of the Fervent Supplication is recited by the Priest, then you should follow his instructions in the biddings of this Litany, just as you did in the Litany which makes up the first part of the Divine Liturgy. How much there is to pray for in this beautiful Litany! For example, think of the almost inexhaustible topics in this bidding for prayer:

> Again we pray for mercy, life, peace, health, salvation, and visitation for the servants of God, and for the pardon and remission of their sins.

If the Prayer of the Ektenia and the prayers of the Catechumens and the Faithful are said in your parish, you may join in saying them with the Priest.

Part Five, the Reading of the Scriptures comes to an end with an abbreviated form of the Shorter Litany which we have learned to expect at the end of all the sections of the Divine Liturgy. According to the Priest's Service Book published in Greece, as well as the practice of many jurisdictions in America, the words, "Help us, save us, have mercy on us; and keep us, O God, by thy Grace" are then repeated. However, in some jurisdictions, notably the Greek Archdiocese of North and South America, these words are omitted.

In each case, though, this Fifth Section of the Divine Liturgy concludes with an ascription which answers the question "How shall we commend ourselves and one another to Christ our God?" even though that portion of the Shorter Litany has also been dropped.

The section ends with the answer to that question: "Grant that ever being protected by thy power, we may ascribe glory to thee; to the Father, the Son, and the Holy Spirit, now and forever and unto ages of ages. Amen."

The reason there is a lack of uniformity in practice at this point in the Divine Liturgy is that the portion following the Gospel Reading is primarily included in the Divine Liturgy for the sake of the Catechumens. The various jurisdictions have responded differently to the fact that we no longer have a class of Catechumens for whom in the past we used to pray, and then asked to leave the Church. Whatever the case, you should conform to the practice in your parish Church. One would hope that the Orthodox Bishops in the United States would come to an acceptable solution to this lack of liturgical uniformity in this country.

In the meantime, the fifth "pearl" has taken its place in the lovely liturgical pendant which is the Divine Liturgy of St. John Chyrsostom. In the next Chapter we continue our description of the Liturgy, with the purpose of guiding you into the practice and experience of true "Life in the Liturgy."

CHAPTER FIVE

Life in the Liturgy (II)

In this Chapter you will learn how to participate specifically and concretely in the balance of the Divine Liturgy, beginning with the Sixth Section which includes the Great Entrance of the Holy Gifts. The Seventh part of the Divine Liturgy, its largest, contains the Great Eucharistic Prayer. The Eighth Section is the Holy Communion, and the Ninth and final section is the Dismissal. Turn your attention, now, to each of these liturgical pearls, where you will find the beauty, meaning, and inspiration of Liturgical Living.

Part Six: The Great Entrance

The Sixth Section now comes into view. The most impressive characteristic of this section is the transfer of the Bread and the Wine from the Table of Preparation, which is located behind the Iconostasis, to the Holy Table. In the Roman Liturgical Tradition, this is done with very little attention or ceremony. In the Liturgies of St. John Chrysostom and St. Basil, however, an important and quite symbolic procession accomplishes the transfer of the Gifts. This transfer of the Chalice, which holds the Wine, and the Paten, which carries the Bread, to the Holy Table is known as the Great Entrance.

The section begins with the singing of a beautiful anthem, the Cherubic Hymn, while the Priest prays penitentially. The Hymn, as we shall shortly see, is interrupted by the Great Entrance Procession. This is followed by the Ektenia (or, The Ektenia of the Prothesis). The word "Ektenia" comes from the Greek word, "Ektenes" which means "extended or long" and it refers to a Litany which, in this case, has for its responses the phrase

"Grant this, O Lord" rather than the usual "Kyrie Eleison." In this case the Shorter Litany is now divided and in between its parts are placed portions of the Ektenia, a longer Litany. The Section concludes with usual ascription.

Let us look at the section a little more carefully. It begins with the Cherubic Hymn. Participation is built into this Hymn. It is written in the second person plural and presupposes your direct participation.

In actuality this is not a hymn of praise directed to God. It is in fact "instruction" given by the choir to the people. The Cherubic Hymn tells us how we ought to participate in the Liturgy at this point of the service.

"We, who mystically represent the Cherubim," the Hymn begins, placing all of the congregation in the role of heavenly angels round about the throne of God. The congregation, as earthly angels are to "sing the Thrice-Holy Hymn" to the life-giving Trinity. In doing this we turn our attention for the time being from the mundane affairs which usually concern us. "Let us put away all worldly care . . ." we sing. And we do this, the Hymn tells us "so that we may receive the King of all." The Lord again is about to come into our presence. Our participation is conditioned by the meaning of the Great Entrance. It is the second symbolic answer to the question, "Why did Christ come into the world?" The first, in the Little Entrance, was that Christ came into the world to teach; the second reason Christ came into the world is now given to us by the Great Entrance—Christ came into the World to die! As the Scriptures say:

> We see Jesus, who was made a little lower than the angels for the suffering of death, crowned with glory and honor; that he by the grace of God should taste death for every man.

The Priest goes to the Altar of the Preparation. In the Greek and other Churches, the Aer or large veil which covers both the Chalice and Paten usually has a Cross embroidered in its center and has two ribbons attached to it. It is tied so that it hangs squarely on the Priest's back. In Russian practice it hangs dramatically

90

over the shoulder. Preceded by the Acolytes then, the Priest lifts the veil-covered Chalice and the Paten and proceeds in procession out of the Altar area into the main Church or Nave which symbolizes the World. Before us, symbolically, Christ again is among us! He bears His Cross on the way to Golgotha. As the Priest reaches the center of the Church, he chants "May the Lord, our God, remember us all in His Kingdom, now and ever, unto ages of ages." These words are clearly reminiscent of the utterance of the penitent thief on the Cross. Christ has come into the world to die for us. The coming real sacramental event of the sacrifice is foreseen here. During the eighteenth century it became the practice at this point to pray for the civic rulers, the Patriarch and Bishops. Some Churches maintain this custom. Some do not. The Priest then goes through the Royal Gate at the center of the Iconostasis and places the Chalice and Paten on the Holy Table. He removes the small veils, censes them and covers the Gifts with the large "Aer."

Before proceeding to indicate how we may participate in this portion of the Divine Liturgy, it is necessary to point to several things about this specific act which are of general importance.

We must be careful to avoid two extremes in the symbolic interpretation of events such as the Great Entrance. On the one hand there is the danger of giving symbolic meaning to these events which is not only completely out of proportion, but which also leads the faithful into wrong practice. For instance, Theodore of Mopsuestia, a writer of Asia Minor who lived around the year 400, interpreted the Great Entrance in his book *Catecheseis* as a procession of angels bearing the already crucified and dead body of the Savior. The body of Christ was understood to be taken to the altar where, upon consecration, it was to be transformed into the *risen* body of Christ. In Mopsuestia's interpretation, the bread and wine, even though unconsecrated, are considered to be the body of our Lord, "holy, awe-inspiring and remote from all corruption, a Body which will very shortly rise to an immortal being." According to one liturgiologist, Dom Gregory Dix, this interpretation became the basis for the practice of some Orthodox to fall down and actually worship the bread and wine as they passed before them in the Great Entrance. This is quite incorrect. Worship is due God alone—the elements in the Great Entrance are bread and wine. After all, the first petition of the litany which follows the Great Entrance clearly says, "for the Precious Gifts here presented," not "and sanctified" as the litany after the Consecration has it. We should not magnify the Great Entrance or any other symbolic act into something more than it is.

A symbolic act represents some event or thing or truth by association, resemblance or convention. It is a deliberate construction designed to give new or more significant meaning to something which would otherwise be of little meaning. Thus Cabasilas sees the Great Entrance as a practical need (to transfer the gifts) but also as a symbol of Christ's Palm Sunday journey "to Jerusalem, where he was to be sacrificed." Archbishop Symeon of Thessalonike seeks to understand it as a representation of "Christ's second coming from the heavens in glory." These interpretations avoid the implications that the elements are to be worshipped. They both emphasize the movement and not the body. The suggested symbolism in this book for the Great Entrance does the same. It suggests that the Great Entrance can be a symbol, representing why Christ came into the world: to die for us. It has the added advantage, lacking in previous interpretations, of fitting into an over-all pattern of the life of Christ as it can be seen in the Divine Liturgy *as it is conducted today.*

This leads us to the other side of the question. As we have already seen, there are numerous liturgiologists who are unhappy with the symbolic interpretation of the Divine Liturgy in any form. Motivated by the historian's concern to describe development of the forms of the Divine Liturgy throughout its history, they tend to see the symbolic interpretation of liturgical practices—such as the Little and Great Entrances—as screens which hide their true history and purpose. They speak as historians of the Liturgy. Thus, they would point to the fact that the Little Entrance was not originally and consciously introduced in the Divine Liturgy to "give us the first reason why Christ came into the world: to teach." In this they are correct. Nor did the Great Entrance come into being historically in a conscious and deliberate way so as to show us "the second reason why Christ came into the world: to die for us."

In actual fact, the Little Entrance was, at a particular point in history, a procession preceding the beginning of the Divine Liturgy. The Patriarch, accompanied by the congregation went to various places outside the Church building. Following the outdoor procession, they began singing the Trisagion Hymn ("Holy God, Holy Mighty, Holy Immortal . . .) as they entered the Church. This was the beginning of the Divine Liturgy. When the outdoor processions stopped, the procession was conducted inside. Later, the idea that the chief liturgist (Patriarch, Archbishop, Bishop, etc.) was officially entering the Altar area behind the iconostasis was emphasized through this procession. At the same time approximately, this Little Entrance was joined with a practical need: to move the Gospel from the Reliquary (skevophylakion) to the Altar Table. Out of these varying historical backgrounds there developed the Little Entrance as we know it now.

A history of the same sort exists for the Great Entrance. It is connected with the old practice of having the Service of the Proskomide or Oblation (the preparation of the bread and wine) between the Liturgy of the Catechumens and the Liturgy of the Faithful. The people brought bread and wine as gifts to a side table in the Church. As the Liturgy of the Faithful was about to begin, after the Catechumens had left, some of the bread and wine was brought from that side table and placed on the Altar. The offering of the bread and wine by the people is no longer a visible liturgical act. Nor is the offering and preparation of the bread and wine by the celebrant.

Thus, in both cases, it was no accident that the Church Fathers began to provide some new symbolic meaning for the liturgical acts which outlived their original historical purposes. Of what value is it for our experience of worship to emphasize that the Little Entrance, for example, arose out of the enjoyment of our Byzantine forebearers in involved processions outside the Church and before the Sacrament began? Or, what spiritual gain is there to be had remembering Sunday after Sunday that the Great Entrance refers to a long dead practice in the liturgical history of the Church?

It is reasonable to hold that the Church in her wisdom and her concern for the spiritual welfare of the Faithful did well to present these events in the Divine Liturgy as symbols which were more edifying and spiritually satisfying in worship than to dwell on "history for history's sake."

Thus, there are two extremes: To overdo what is obviously symbolic, on the one hand, and to ignore it on the other. In the growing and developing tradition of the Church, the edification of the Faithful has a high priority. It is with this sense of values that many Fathers and spiritual writers have sought to make the actions of the Divine Liturgy more spiritually rewarding by providing symbolic meanings for them. In the judgment of the author of this book, both participation and devotion are increased by this practice. And that justifies it.

With that behind us, let us now see how we can better participate in the section of the Divine Liturgy now under discussion.

How do you participate in this Great Entrance? Obviously, the several ways we have already pointed out are readily available to you. You can sing along or subsing with the choir as they sing the Cherubic Hymn. Or, if you wish you can say its words slowly and meditatively to yourself as you listen to the music. In addition, you can use its thoughts and words as a theme for an extended prayer of your own.

While the choir sings the Cherubic Hymn you can,

if you wish, recite the penitential "prayer of the Cherubic Hymn" together with the Priest, and as the Priest censes the people after this prayer, you can repeat with him David's prayer for forgiveness, the 50th (51st) Psalm. In fact you should know that this is primarily the place where the Priest confesses his own sins and his unworthiness before God. It is the ideal place for the layman to do the same thing. In the Divine Liturgy of St. John Chrysostom we do not have a public confession of our sins. You should take this opportunity to think of what you have done during the past week which was not pleasing to God nor fitting in the life of a Christian. "Have I harmed another?" "Have I spoken in an unchristian manner to friend or relative or co-worker?" "Have I failed to do what I should have done as a follower of Christ?" "Did I fail to show love when it was needed?" Ask yourself these and similar questions. Confess your sins. Ask God for pardon. The Priest is doing the same thing as he censes the Church and the people. When the Priest censes in your direction bow your head, making the sign of the Cross in acknowledgement of your sharing in the prayer and action of the Divine Liturgy and as a sign of repentance for your sins. The Priest will then bow toward the congregation, asking for your forgiveness. Bow your head as you grant that forgiveness and ask for forgiveness yourself.

When the Great Entrance takes place, Christ is bearing His Cross for us, in our mind's eye. We are part of the crowd on the *via Dolorosa*, the "way of sorrows" which Christ travelled as He went to His crucifixion. We deliberately "put away all worldly care." We open our hearts that "we may receive the King of all" as He comes into *our* world to die for us. What would you have felt in your heart if you had been there then? Unworthiness? Wonder? Love? Gratitude? All these are appropriate responses at this moment of liturgical action. Christ is come into the world to die for you and for all people. He is before us. How do you respond? Perhaps no better way can be found than to pray with the Priest "May the Lord, our God, remember us all in His

Kingdom, now and ever and unto ages of ages. Amen."
We commend not only ourselves but also one another.
It is not selfish, it is corporate. Our sins have brought
Him here; His presence here has redeemed us all of our
sins; together we are members of His Kingdom.
The choir then completes the Cherubic Hymn which
was interrupted by the Great Entrance. Previously the
choir prayed "that we may receive the King of all . . ."
Now the choir continues speaking of the King who
comes "invisibly attended by the angelic hosts. Alleluia,
Alleluia, Alleluia."
The word "Alleluia" means "let us praise the Lord."
Like the word "Amen," it has not been translated from
the original Hebrew. One commentator describes it as

> a cry for joy. Alleluia faithfully expresses the loving grati-
> tude, praise and admiration of Him whom angels and
> archangels, the cherubim and seraphim praise in the
> splendors of heaven.

Participation in the "Alleluia" means repeating the
words with the choir in an exalting, joyful, grateful mood.
The Ektenia follows: "Let us complete our prayer
to the Lord." The Priest calls on us to pray "for the
precious gifts now offered"; "for this holy House and
for those who enter it with faith, reverence, and the fear
of God"; and he asks us to pray for our "deliverance
from all tribulation, wrath, danger, and necessity."
Each time, the choir responds with the words, "Lord,
have mercy." Each of us should pray for the gifts, that
in time they may be accepted by the Lord, for our fellow worshippers, and for our freedom from evil and
troublesome events in our lives.
This is followed by the familiar "Help us, save us,
have mercy on us, and protect us, O God, by thy
grace." We would expect, from our past experience, to
have this immediately followed by the usual phrase
"Commemorating our most Holy, pure . . ." But this is
not the case. The principle of theme and variations takes
affect again. Sandwiched between these two familiar
phrases is the Ektenia which is also often referred to

as the "Spiritual Litany." Its concerns reflect the fact that we *have* put away "all worldly care." The Priest calls upon the congregated body of Christ to pray for the "whole day that it may be perfect and holy, peaceful and sinless;" for an "angel of peace" who will guide and protect us, for "the forgiveness of our sins;" for "things good and profitable for our souls;" that "the end of our lives may be Christian without torment, blameless and peaceful;" and that when our time comes to die it may be in faith so that we need not fear the Judgment to come.

After we have prayed for these things quietly within us, participating actively in this Litany also, we then hear the Priest intoning the familiar phrase, "Commemorating our most Holy, pure, blessed, and glorified Lady, the Mother of God and Ever-Virgin Mary, with all the Saints." He again urges us to "commend ourselves and one another and our whole life to Christ our God." In practice this is then followed immediately with the ascription which this time again answers the question "How, or, in what manner shall we commend ourselves and one another to God?" "Through the compassion of Thine only begotten Son . . ." is the answer. And thus the Sixth Section—the Great Entrance—comes to an end. In it Christ has appeared, revealing to us the second reason He came into the world: to die for us. The bread and wine have been transferred to the Holy Altar Table. Everything is ready now for the key portion of the Divine Liturgy. We have prayed for many things in the Litany. We have sung hymns to God in the second and third parts of the Liturgy. We have received Christ as Teacher and heard His Teaching in the fourth and fifth sections of the Divine Liturgy. In the sixth part we have received the Lord who came to sacrifice Himself for us and we have brought the bread and wine in solemn and penitential procession to the Altar Table. We are at the sacramental heart of the Divine Liturgy!

Part Seven: The Great Eucharistic Prayer

We are now about to enter the Seventh Section of the

Divine Liturgy. This section is the largest and sacramentally speaking, the most important and most ancient part of the Liturgy. Up to this point, if you think back, we have done very little that is directly related with the performance of the Sacrament itself. Other than transfering the Bread and the Wine from the Prothesis to the Holy Table, little if anything can be directly related to the action of the preparation, consecration, and distribution of the elements of the Sacrament. Though certainly, *we* have been prepared for the sacrament by what has preceded.

This is not to say that the first Six Sections were not sacramentally necessary for as we have seen, prayers, Scripture Readings, Hymns, and Sermon go back to the very beginnings of our Christian Liturgical Tradition. They serve to prepare *us*. What we do in making this observation is to point out that in the Seventh Section of the Liturgy we turn our attention primarily to the elements of the Sacrament. Since most of these acts take place in a long and ancient prayer known as the "Great Eucharistic Prayer" of which we will speak later, we name the whole Seventh Section after this Great Eucharistic Prayer.

This section consists of several portions which invite our participation in the Liturgy in many various ways. The Seventh "unit" begins with a blessing and ends with a blessing. The initial blessing is followed by a brief sung affirmation of faith in the Holy Trinity. The recitation of the Creed follows. There is then a liturgical dialogue in which our attention is drawn to the fact that we are about to enter into the most sacred part of the Divine Liturgy. This is followed by the Great Eucharistic Prayer, parts of which are said aloud by the Priest, parts of which are said inaudibly by the Priest, and parts of which are sung by the choir and people. It is, however, one long prayer. This is followed by another Ektenia, expanded to include the Lord's Prayer and the final blessing. It concludes with the usual ascription to the Trinity which we have now become accustomed to seeing at the end of a section.

The section thus begins with a *blessing*: "Peace be to all." The laity bow their heads to receive the blessing and then return the blessing with the words, "And with thy spirit." Then, a brief dialogue takes place during which the Priest calls upon you to "Love one another"; this so that we might be unified as the body of Christ and thus "with one mind confess..." What? Here the choir finishes the Priest's sentence for him. Let us confess "Father, Son, and Holy Spirit; Trinity, One in substance and Undivided." This is in actuality a call to repeat the Creed.

It is at this point, just before the Creed, which is the sign of our unity in Faith, that the ancient Christian custom of the *Kiss of Peace* took place. Our unity in love is both the result of our unity in Faith and the presupposition of our sincere confession of faith in God who is love. As Gogol points out, "For if we do not love one another it is impossible to love Him who is all pure love, complete and perfect." Unfortunately, this beautiful liturgical practice showing the unity of Christians has all but disappeared from our Service. The only remnant of it is the reverencing of the Gifts by the Priest; and, when the Priest co-celebrates with another Priest and in pontifical Liturgies, the Kiss of Peace is exchanged by the clergy. Certainly each Christian in attendance can at least affirm his love for all other Christians at this point.

We then hear something strange and peculiar just before the Creed. At this most holy and touching moment the Priest chants "The Doors! The Doors! In wisdom let us attend! It seems to be out of place. Yet Panagio-topoulos explains:

> In the ancient Church the first of these exclamations was directed to the door-keepers who stood at the door of the Church building and whose task it was to see to it that no unbeliever should enter the Church. And since at this moment on the one hand the Creed was recited and on the other, the veiled Holy Gifts were uncovered and the sanctification was about to take place, the Deacons called the attention of the door-keepers to their

duties that they might discharge them properly . . . the second exclamation "In wisdom, let us attend" is an explanation of the first. By this we are called to attend carefully to the confession of faith which we are about to offer before God. As an act of devotion and worship we are urged to pay careful attention "in wisdom," that is, paying attention to the meaning of the Creed with full understanding of its truth and its supreme meaning and significance."

We note that this same interpretation is recorded also in the description of the ancient liturgy in the *Constitutions of the Holy Apostles.* " . . . let the door be watched, lest any unbeliever, or one not yet initiated, come in." It is a reminder to you that generations of Christians risked their lives for this Faith, not only in the past history, but even today. It is a serious business to repeat the Creed of Faith of the Orthodox Christian Church! Participation in the Creed means, then, not only that we say it together with the Priest, acolyte, chantor or choir—whoever it is that leads the recitation of it in our parish Church—but that we also do it prayerfully, in a spirit of devotion and utter seriousness. You can make it even more meaningful if you do not simply recite it, but rather direct the words of the Creed to God. Tell God what you believe!

After the recitation of the Creed the Priest again calls the worshippers to attention: "Let us stand aright; let us stand in awe; let us attend . . ." The reason for this intensive call to attentiveness is that the central act of our Eucharistic worship is about to begin. We are about to "make the Holy Offering." The choir responds with the names of the highest forms of the ancient Hebrew sacrifice, the Peace Offering, and *its* highest form, the Thank Offering. The Apostolic blessing follows as the Priest blesses the people with the Cross uttering the same blessing given by the Apostle Paul to the Christians of Corinth.

> The Grace of our Lord, Jesus Christ, and the Love of God, the Father, and the Communion of the Holy Spirit, be with you all.

You participate by bowing your head and, if you choose, by making the sign of the Cross. You might also pray that you be open to and worthy of this blessing. In turn, the laity blesses the Priest returning his blessing with the words "And with thy spirit." The Priest then raises his eyes and hands upward and calls upon all to "lift up our hearts" to the Lord. In this liturgical dialogue the worshippers respond together with the choir "We lift them up unto the Lord" and thus place themselves far removed from the concerns of the world. We are wholly ready to enter into the Eucharist proper. The Priest turns to the Icon of Christ and invites you to give thanks to the Lord through the Mystery of the Eucharist itself. "Eucharistisomen to Kyrio" are the words in the original Greek. "Let us give thanks unto the Lord," he says. The Choir and people respond affirmatively, "It is meet and right." It is proper that we should do this. Some liturgical texts expand on this saying, "It is meet and right to worship the Father, the Son, and the Holy Spirit; the Trinity, One in Essence, and Undivided." Thus the blessing, the Creed, and the Apostolic dialogue are completed and the Great Eucharistic prayer begins.

As the choir sings "It is meet and right" the Priest begins the *Great Eucharistic Prayer* with the very same words ... "It is meet and right to hymn thee, to bless thee, to praise thee ..." The Great Eucharistic Prayer does five specific things as it is said inaudibly and audibly by the Priest and as it is sung by the choir. It, above all, gives thanks. Secondly, it remembers, "Do this in remembrance of Me," Jesus said, including the words by which Christ established the Sacrament, the words of Institution. The third thing which the Great Eucharistic Prayer does is to make the offering of the Bread and Wine to God. This is followed by the consecration of the Bread and Wine in which the Lord is called to consecrate the elements, making them the very Body and Blood of the Crucified and Risen Savior. The fifth thing which the Great Eucharistic Prayer does is to commemorate those for whom the sacrifice is offered.

While all of these acts are essentially sacramental acts, needing no further meaning than their real and direct part in the sacramental action, they also serve as reminders of those events in the life of Christ which are intimately related to His saving work. The sacramental action here is dominant and in the forefront. But the symbolism of the life of Christ stands quietly in the background. Symbolism is now overshadowed by sacramental reality, but it is still there, an additional source of enrichment for our participation in the Divine Liturgy.

Let us now carefully examine the Great Eucharistic Prayer with the emphasis on our participation in this, the very heart and core of the Divine Liturgy. The best way to begin participation here is to read the beginning of the prayer with the Priest in a spirit of thankfulness. As you pray you count God's blessings first, those which you know and those which you do not know.

Priest (inaudibly): It is meet and right to praise Thee, to glorify Thee, to bless Thee, to give thanks to Thee, to worship Thee, in all places of Thy dominion, for Thou art God ineffable, incomprehensible, inconceiveable, existing always as Thou dost exist, Thou and Thine only-begotten Son, and Thy Holy Spirit. Thou hast brought us from nothingness into being, and when we fell away didst raise us up again, and Thou ceaseth not until Thou hast done everything to bring us to Heaven, and confer on us Thy Kingdom to come. For all these things we give thanks to Thee and to Thine only-begotten Son and to Thy Holy Spirit, for all the things we know and do not know, for the seen and the unseen benefits which we enjoy.

The worshipping Christians offer their thanks even though the angels thank, praise, and glorigy God.

We render thanks to Thee also for this Service which Thou dost deign to receive at our hands, though Thou art surrounded by thousands of Archangels and tens of thousands of Angels, by the Cherubim and Seraphim that are six-winged, full of eyes and soar aloft on their wings.

All this the Priest says silently. And then, aloud, continuing the Prayer and in reference to the Angelic

102

Hosts round about the throne of God, the Priest describes them as "singing, voicing, proclaiming, and saying the triumphal hymn."

At this point the choir takes over the prayer. They begin singing the Hymn referred to by Isaiah in the description of the heavenly vision of the Angels round the heavenly throne which we find in the sixth chapter of the Old Testament book of Isaiah:

> Holy, Holy, Holy, Lord of Hosts, heaven and earth are full of Thy glory: Hosanna in the highest: Blessed is He that cometh in the Name of the Lord. Hosanna in the highest.

You can participate at this point by joining in the Hymn, by subsinging, or contemplating its content. Yet, perhaps reading along with the Priest here is the best way. As the choir begins to sing, the Priest continues the prayer again inaudibly showing our identification with the angels and moving to the "Remembrance." With a general reference to the whole saving work of Christ and with words reminiscent of John 3:16, he introduces a wide-brush-stroke sketch of the divine Economy of salvation:

> Priest (inaudibly): We also, O merciful Master, with these celestial Powers cry and say: Holy art Thou and All-Holy, Thou and Thy only-begotten Son and Thy Holy Spirit. Holy art Thou and All-Holy and sublime is Thy Glory: Thou Who didst so love Thy word that Thou gavest Thine only-begotten Son, that whoso believeth on Him should not perish but have everlasting Life.

As these words are repeated we remember with gratitude what God has done. Then the prayer proceeds to the remembrance of specific events. The first thing we remember specifically is the Last Supper:

> And when He had come and had fulfilled all that was needed for us, in the same night in which He was betrayed, or rather in which He gave Himself up for the Life of the World, He took bread in His holy, pure and blameless Hands, and when He had given thanks and blessed and hallowed, He brake it and gave it to His holy Disciples and Apostles, saying:

He then repeats the words of Institution by which Christ ordered the establishment of this rite as an act for and by the Church:

Priest: Take ye, eat: This is My Body, Which for you is broken, unto remission of sins.

Choir: Amen.

Priest (inaudibly): Likewise after Supper the Cup, saying: (Aloud) Drink of it ye all: This is My Blood, of the New Testament, Which for you and for many is shed, unto the remission of sins.

Choir: Amen.

We are present at the Last Supper in reality and also symbolically. As these words take us down the corridor of time, we are mystically present in that upper room. It is as if we are sitting together with the disciples. The same words ring in our ears as in theirs. What do you feel? What do you see? Raise your eyes to the Icon of the Mystical Supper over the Royal Gate of the Iconostasis. You are one with the disciples as they look upon the Master's face. What can you say? Shall you not reverence yourself and bow your head praising God for His outpouring of love, for His forgiveness of your sins and those of all mankind? Do you not sense His divine Presence before us and humbly from the depths of your heart utter in all humility "Glory to Thee, O God, Glory to Thee"?

The Priest concludes the remembrance. In staccato-like phrases the highlights of that whole life, given for the salvation of the world, are rehearsed:

Priest (inaudibly): Commemorating this command of our Saviour and all that was endured for our sake, the Cross, the Grave, the Resurrection after three days, the Ascension into Heaven the Enthronement at the right hand of the Father, and the second and glorious Coming again.

We have thanked; we have remembered, we now offer the Bread and Wine to God. With crossed hands the Priest lifts up our gifts, the Bread and Wine in their sacred Vessels and offers them to God. But look at the paradox! What we offer is not really ours. It belongs to God since all Creation is His. The Bread and Wine is simply a portion, a token return of His gifts to us! As the Priest does this on our behalf he says:

> Thy gifts of what is Thine, do we offer to Thee, in all we do and for all Thy Blessings.

It is all of us who make this offering through the Priest. However, it was Christ who first made the offering of Himself in the Garden of Gethsemane, "Not my will, but Thy will be done," He prayed as He offered Himself willingly on behalf of the world. He offered Himself. We offer the Bread and Wine which, as we have seen, symbolize the Church gathered together in the imagery of St. Cyprian. And so the choir breaks in with a Hymn of deep and moving adoration.

> We praise Thee, we bless Thee, we give thanks unto Thee, O Lord, and we entreat Thee, O our God.

Certainly it is appropriate to join in this hymn by sub-singing, or to meditate on the Lord's agony in the Garden of Gethsemane. The Priest, however, continues the Great Eucharistic Prayer carrying it on to the next portion, the Consecration. Here the Priest asks God to send His Holy Spirit upon the Bread and upon the Wine in the Chalice, nd to make them the Precious Body of Christ and the Precious Blood of Christ.

Now the Crucified Lord as the Sacrificed Lamb of the world, is before us. As Cabasilas so dramatically puts it:

> When these words have been said, the whole sacred rite has been accomplished, the offerings are consecrated, the sacrifice is complete; the splendid Victim, the Divine Oblation, slain for the salvation of the world, lies upon the Altar.

How do we react to this event? What is our mode and manner of participation? The moment of Consecration is the presence of the Crucified before us. In some Orthodox Churches the Christians kneel here, not in prayer for forgiveness, but in adoration before the Crucified One! Our eyes may seek out the Icon of the Crucifixion over the top of the Iconostasis, or behind the Holy

Altar Table. You are gathered together with the devoted disciples at the foot of the Cross of Calvary. We do not sense terror or sorrow; rather we know that this is the supreme act of Love which leads to our true life, in that "he died for all, that those who live might live no longer for themselves, but for Him who for their sake died and was raised" in the words of the Bible. In the background the choir is singing the hymn which expresses our mood of gratitude and outpouring love for Him who profoundly and deeply loved us.

Make this most sacred of moments your own. Imagine yourself at the foot of His Holy Cross. Thank and glorify the Savior for His great Love; sing with the choir; meditate on God's great Love. It was for you that He came to die!

The Great Eucharistic Prayer, now comes to its last part. For whom is this sacrifice offered? As the Hymn above comes to its conclusion the Priest offers the Eucharist in the first instance for those who are about to receive Holy Communion and for their benefit:

> So that They may be to those that receive Them for the purification of the soul, for the remission of sins, for the Fellowship of thy Holy Spirit, for the fulfillment of the Kingdom of Heaven, and for boldness to approach Thee neither unto judgment nor unto condemnation.

It is secondly offered for the Saints and Holy ones who have gone before us; "Patriarchs, Prophets, Apostles, Preachers, Evangelists, Martyrs, Confessors, Ascetics, and every righteous spirit made perfect in faith." And then aloud the Priest begins to mention individual Saints of special note for whom the Sacrament has been offered. The Theotokos is at the head of this list of Saints especially mentioned.

> Especially our all holy, immaculate, most blessed and glorious Lady, the Mother of God and Ever-Virgin, Mary.

The choir in the name of the people interrupts the prayer, so to speak, with a Hymn of enthusiastic approval. "That is a good idea!" the choir seems to say, and it is followed by the singing of praises to the Mother of God for whom, also, the Divine Liturgy has been offered. "It is truly meet to bless thee O Theotokos . . ." As the choir sings this, the Priest continues to pray and to mention other specific Saints: St. John the Forerunner, the Apostles, and the Saint of the day. After those who are to commune, the Saints in general and in particular, the Priest offers the Sacrifice for the faithful who have died in the hope of the Resurrection. The Sacrament is also offered for the Clergy, for the whole world, for the Holy and Apostolic Church, for the pious, for the civil rulers and the defense forces. All of these petitions are said inaudibly while the praise of the Theotokos is being sung. When this is over, the Priest continues aloud to mention for whom the Sacrament is offered, mentioning by name the Bishop, Metropolitan, or Archbishop, under whose jurisdiction the parish exists. Then again inaudibly he continues to mention those for whom the Sacrament is offered; the city where the parish is located; as well as every city and land; those who travel; the sick, suffering, the captives; those who work in the Churches proper; the poor; and all of us.

The Sacrament has been offered for all and everyone! The Great Eucharistic Prayer comes to an end. As the Priest prays you should join with him in his prayerful expression of the intentions of all of the gathered Faithful; truly an ecumenical prayer! The Priest concludes the Great Eucharistic Prayer with an appeal that this unity may be always realized in our praise of God:

> And grant that in one voice and one heart we may glorify and praise Thy sublime and majestic Name of the Father and of the Son and of the Holy Spirit, now and ever and unto ages of ages.

But this is not the end of this great and important section of the Divine Liturgy. Just as the Great Eucharistic Prayer was preceded by certain portions of the section, it is also followed by several additional elements. The Ektenia is repeated. Preceding it is a blessing reminiscent of the previous Apostolic blessing.

> And the mercies of the Great God and our Savior Jesus Christ be with you all.

107

We now expect to hear the ascription which we are accustomed to seeing in this place, but the variation again comes into play. Before the Great Eucharistic Prayer we recited the Creed. After it, we recite the Lord's Prayer.

It is introduced with words which challenge us in the temptation to thoughtlessly repeat the words of the prayer. The Priest asks that we may fully understand how bold we are when we dare to call upon the Creator, the Transcendent Maker of all that is, and the Author of our existence as "Father."

The congregation accepts the blessing with the bowing of the head and returns the blessing with the words "And with thy spirit" directed toward the Priest. The Litany begins with the usual call to prayer in a slightly varied form:

> Having commemorated all the saints, again and again, let us pray to the Lord.

The Faithful are then called upon to pray specifically for the consecrated gifts, that is, that God receive them at His heavenly spiritual Altar and, in return, send down to us divine Grace. You should make these words over into your own prayer. Again the familiar words which signal the ending of a section are heard:

> Help, save, comfort, and protect us, O God, by thy Grace.

But again the principle of theme and variations is applied. The petitions of the Ektenia now call us to pray that the day might be perfect; for an angel of peace; for the forgiveness of our sins; for things good and profitable for our soul; for the peace of the world; for the reverent and pious living of the rest of our earthly days; and for a Christian ending to our lives. It is here that the next expected phrase of the Little Litany appears, but in a slightly variant form. Instead of beginning with the words, "Commemorating our most Holy, pure, blessed and glorified Lady, Mother of God and Ever-Virgin Mary . . ." the Priest says:

> Asking for the unity of the Faith, and the communion of the Holy Spirit, let us commend ourselves and one another and our whole life unto Christ our God.

We now expect to hear the ascription which we are accustomed to seeing in this place, but the variation again comes into play. Before the Great Eucharistic Prayer we recited the Creed. After it, we recite the Lord's Prayer.

It is introduced with words which challenge us in the temptation to thoughtlessly repeat the words of the prayer. The Priest asks that we may fully understand how bold we are when we dare to call upon the Creator, the Transcendent Maker of all that is, and the Author of our existence as "Father."

Together we recite the Lord's Prayer. Is it necessary to point out the need to do so with comprehension and sincere feeling and meaningfulness? Cabasilas notes that "The whole congregation says the prayer with him (the Priest), and the Priest raises his voice when he comes to the end and recites the conclusion as a doxology."

As this section began with a blessing, it now ends with the same blessing. "Peace by with you all" the Priest says, the Faithful returning the blessing with the words, "and to thy spirit." After this great expression of God's loving acts to us, the Priest then calls upon all to bow their heads unto the Lord and we all bow in the direction of the Icon of Christ on the Iconostasis acknowledging Him as Lord. In the words of Cabasilas, the worshippers

> bow before Him not simply as creatures before their Lord and Creator, but as purchased slaves to Him who obtained them at the price of the blood of His only Son; for He possesses us by double right, as slaves whom He has made His children.

Give yourself heart and soul to this liturgical action, recognizing God's goodness to you through Christ Jesus.

With this, a silent prayer of thanksgiving is read by the Priest and concluded with the ascription to the Trinity which we have seen always concludes a section of the Liturgy. It also provides us with another way in which we can "commend ourselves and one another to Christ our God."

> Through the grace and mercy and love for men of
> Thine Only-Begotten Son, with whom Thou art blessed,

with Thine All-holy, and good, and life-giving Spirit, now and ever and unto ages of ages. Amen.

With this, the largest section of the Liturgy is completed. It is the "great pearl" in the pendant of the Divine Liturgy. It is the heart of the Liturgical action. It provides you with a whole range of opportunities to participate in worship: litanies, blessings, dialogues, symbolism, purely sacramental action, recitation, and hymn-singing. Take advantage of these opportunities. It is followed by only two more sections. The Eighth Section is the Communion.

Part Eight: The Communion

This section or "unit" of the Liturgy begins with words which call the Faithful to attention, "Let us attend!" And then a warning comes: "Holy things are for the holy." The Priest says this reflecting the words of the Lord that pearls are not to be thrown down before the swine to trample upon. But, if this is the case, you are entitled to ask, "who *is* worthy, who *is* holy enough to approach the Chalice and partake of the Body and Blood of the Lord?" The choir—as if reaching out its hand and tapping the Priest's shoulder with a friendly reminder—intimates that there is only One who measures up to that requirement:

One is Holy, One is Lord, Jesus Christ, to the Glory of God, the Father. Amen.

This hymn encourages you to plan to receive Holy Communion as frequently as possible. None of us is really worthy, yet all are invited to commune with the Lord and to become one with Him through the Holy Sacrament of the Eucharist. Pray that you might always be accepted as a communicant of His Chalice.

The Priest first receives Holy Communion as the choir sings the Communion Anthem "Praise ye the Lord from the heavens; Praise Him in the Highest. Alleluia."

The Priest then prepares the elements and himself for Communion. He breaks the Consecrated Bread and places a portion in the Chalice. Then he blesses a cup of boiling water; he likens it to the zeal and enthusiasm

110

of the Saints, which is symbolically joined with Christ, as the water is poured into the Chalice also. The Priest follows the preparation of the Chalice with a preparation of himself, through the reading of a number of prayers before Holy Communion. Some or all of these prayers may be included in the Service Book used in your jurisdiction. Then the Priest approaches the Paten and consumes a portion of the Body of Christ. He lifts the Chalice and drinks of the Blood of Christ. Having kissed the Chalice, he repeats prayers of Thanksgiving, while at the same time he places the particles of the Lord's Body into the Holy Chalice.

You can participate in this portion of the Divine Liturgy by subsinging with the choir, reading the prayers of the Priest as he communes, and reading the prayers before Holy Communion, especially if you are planning to Commune. These prayers are essentially the same for both Clergy and laity.

In most Churches the Royal Gates are closed at this point while the Priest is receiving Communion. In Churches with more than one Priest sometimes this is the point where the Sermon is preached. When he has completed his own Communion, the doors are opened, and the Priest comes forward with the Chalice raised high. It is as if the rock has been moved away from the tomb and the Resurrected Lord now comes toward us. The New Life of Christ is offered to you and all the Faithful. The Priest calls those who are prepared to approach the Source of Life, Jesus Christ who is the Victor over death, and sin, and evil.

With fear of God, with faith, and with love, draw near.

Here is the most important, most real, and profound way of participating in the Divine Liturgy: Holy Communion! This is true participation, real worship, actual sharing and union. It should not be a rare practice. You should seek to be a frequent communicant at the Banquet of the Lord. If you are receiving Holy Communion that day, leave your place reverently and approach the Chalice in a prayerful attitude. You may continue to pray the "Prayers Before Holy Communion" if you wish. Or, you may make this most personal moment of Communion with God an opportunity to speak to the Lord with the most intimate and personal words of prayer. As you approach to receive your Lord, do so with the realization that you are about to be united with Christ, "who loves us and has freed us from our sins by His Blood and made us a kingdom, priests to his God and Father."

After receiving the Holy Mysteries, you should return to your place. Your mood, if not your exact words should parallel those of St. Paul who said: "It is no longer I who live, but Christ who lives in me; and the life I now live in the flesh, I live by faith in the Son of God, who loved me and gave himself for me." There are a number of Thanksgiving Prayers which you may read from your Service Book at this point.

If, however, you do not receive Holy Communion, you can still do a number of things. You should individually pray for those who are receiving, you can contemplate the meaning of God's love for you, your fellow worshippers and all the world, or you may join the choir in singing the Communion Hymn.

After Communion the Priest raises the Chalice and says:

"O God, save Thy people and bless Thine heritage."

It is in Holy Communion that we become truly the people of God and His inheritance.

The Laity now express the joy of the Faithful at this participation in the new life, in witness to the Resurrection of the Lord, and in sharing in the very Body and Blood of Christ.

We have seen the pure Light, we have received the Heavenly Spirit, we have found the true Faith, worshipping the Undivided Trinity, who hath saved us!

Participate by subsinging this joyful and triumphant hymn, making its words your own. In the meantime the Priest censes the Gifts saying inaudibly

"Be Thou exalted, O God, above the heavens, and Thy glory above all the earth."

He then lifts the Chalice and Paten high as if to show

the Ascension of our Lord into the heavens and he blesses the people with the Chalice and Paten before he returns them to the Preparation Table. As he does this, the Priest prays inaudibly, "Blessed is our God," and then aloud, "Always now and ever and unto ages of ages." The Priest returns to the Holy Table. The section now ends, as is usual, with the Shorter Litany in a variant form.

Help, save, have mercy and protect us, O Lord, by Thy grace.

Entreating the Lord that this whole day may be perfect, holy, peaceful and sinless, let us commend ourselves and one another, and our while life to Christ, our God.

With these now familiar words, we realize that this Eighth and next-to-last section of the Divine Liturgy is concluded. We are given yet another reason "why" we should "commend ourselves and one another" to Christ. We have just received Holy Communion, so we give ourselves over to the Lord because He is "Our Sanctification." The eighth pearl, "The Holy Communion," has been placed on the string of our beautiful liturgical pendant. There remains one more pearl which provides the last jewel: "The Dismissal."

Part Nine: "The Dismissal"

The final section of the Divine Liturgy of St. John Chrysostom takes its theme from the Priest's words of instruction to the Faithful: "Let us go forth in peace, praying to the Lord." Pray, then, with the choir, as it sings, "Lord have mercy," three times and then join them in calling upon your Priest with the words, "Holy father, give the blessing."

The Priest responds to that invitation with a prayer said in front of the Icon of Christ. It is known as the "prayer from behind the ambon (pulpit)." At one time, many centuries ago, the pulpit was in the center of the Church and the preacher spoke in all directions to the people who stood around him. At this point in the Divine Liturgy, it seems that the Priest moved from the Holy

Table to the foot of the Pulpit. Thus, he stood in the middle of all the worshippers. Turning toward the Altar, he spoke from among the people on their behalf:

O Lord, who blessest those who bless Thee and sanctifiest those who put their trust in Thee, save Thy people and bless Thine heritage; protect the whole body of Thy Church, and sanctify those who love the beauty of Thy House.

Today, this prayer is said by the Priest in front of the icon of Christ at the Iconostasis, but it still is a prayer said in the name of, and in behalf of the whole body of Christ, the Church.

As the Priest prays for you, open your heart to receive God's blessings. Remember, that more than ever, at this moment, in this place, together with all the other Faithful Orthodox Christians, you are "the people of God"; you are "sons and daughters in the household of God"; you are "His Body"; you are "The Church." Join the Priest, then, as he completes this prayer, praying with him for the peace of the world, and all who are in it, recognizing that "every perfect gift is from above." To this affirmation there is only one possible response. Join the choir singing joyfully, gratefully, and confidently these words of praise:

Blessed be the Name of the Lord, from this time forth and forever more.

The Priest blesses the Faithful for a final time and concludes by calling upon all the Saints, including the Saint whose memory is celebrated on that day, to intercede for us before Christ. Make the sign of the Cross, receiving the blessings and intercessions of the Saints on your behalf.

In some Churches the choir sings a prayer on behalf of the Priest while he recites this final prayer: "Protect, O Lord, unto many years him who blesseth us and bringeth us Thy grace." Would it not be appropriate for you to also offer a prayer with your own words for your parish Priest?

The Divine Liturgy concludes with the same words

which conclude every other Orthodox Christian Service: "Through the prayers of our holy Fathers have mercy upon us, O Lord Jesus Christ, our God." Some commentators hold that the "holy Fathers" referred to are the great Fathers of the Church, such as St. John Chrysostom, St. Basil, St. Gregory, etc. Others, however, see this phrase coming out of monastic practice where "holy Fathers" refers to all the members of the monastic community. In a parish setting these words would actually be saying "Through the prayers of all the Faithful gathered there, have mercy on us, O Lord Jesus Christ, our God." Whatever the case, it is the members of the Church praying for the other members of the Church. In this spirit of mutual concern, love, and common prayer that the Divine Liturgy ends.

"Amen" the choir says. "So be it," we all agree. After the Service, the Faithful file before the Priest and receive a cube of bread from the Priest. In Greek this is known as "Antidoron"—"instead of the Gift." The Altar boys have cut this bread from the loaves of offering bread from which the Priest previously removed the portion which was ultimately consecrated and made the Body and Blood of our Lord. What remains of the loaves is distributed to the Faithful. It is blessed, but not consecrated. In a sense, all those present thus share in the meal aspect of the Holy Eucharist through the Antidoron. As you receive the blessed bread, pray that God will always make you worthy to be present and to share in this most unique of Services—the celebration of the Mystery of the Eucharist!

CHAPTER SIX

Making the Liturgy Live

The preceding chapters have sought to help you participate more actively, conscientiously, and more knowledgeably in the Divine Liturgy. In the Fourth and Fifth Chapters, just concluded, you were given insights and suggestions regarding the specific ways by which you can share in the Divine Liturgy. Now, in this final chapter, you will find the text of the Service, divided in the nine parts identified in this book—together with brief instructions which suggest to you how to make your attendance at the Divine Liturgy an inspiring and meaningful experience.

In order to make the reading of this book worthwhile, you must now begin putting into practice what you have learned. The handbook in this chapter will help you do just that. You should take this book with you to Church this coming Sunday and for at least a month afterwards. Go from the beginning with the intent of putting yourself into the life of the Liturgy. Follow the instructions for each of the sections. Use your own words as you pray on the various themes presented to you. Bring your concerns and interests from your family, home, school, work, social, intellectual, emotional and even political life. Involve your life with the life of the Liturgy. Make the Liturgy live for you!

You will only begin to "get something out of the Liturgy" when you begin "putting yourself into the Liturgy." This will happen from the very first. However, as the weeks and months go by, you will discover that the experiences you gain and share with your fellow Christians in worship will become more and more varied and rich. New insights and new expressions will begin to come to you as gifts from God. To be sure, there will also be "dry" days when you will find it very difficult to pray actively and to share energetically in the Service. Do not be discouraged. For those who persist, these are only passing experiences and are quickly replaced by more satisfying and meaningful participation.

But you will never understand the joy of "Living the Liturgy" until you do it! Familiarize yourself, now, with the text of the Divine Liturgy as it is presented in the pages that follow. Take this book with you to Church next Sunday. Use it in accordance with what you have learned in a devout and reverent spirit. Persist in this, following the instructions in the text for at least one month or so. Then, ask yourself where you stand liturgically. Is not the Divine Liturgy a more meaningful, inspiring, living and vital experience for you? If you have done what we have said here, it is virtually inevitable that your answer will be in the affirmative. Then, you can be sure that you will have a lifetime of rich worship experiences before you because you will, in truth, be "Living the Liturgy!"

The Divine Liturgy of St. John Chrysostom

PRIEST: Blessed be the Kingdom of the Father and of the Son and of the Holy Spirit, now and ever and unto ages of ages.
LAITY: Amen.

Part One: The Litany

The Priest calls upon you to pray for numerous things. You should participate in the Liturgy by silently praying for each of these things.

PRIEST: In peace let us entreat the Lord.
LAITY: Lord, have mercy.
PRIEST: For the peace from above and the salvation of our souls, let us entreat the Lord.
LAITY: Lord, have mercy.
PRIEST: For the peace of the whole world, for the stability of the Holy Churches of God, and for the union of all, let us entreat the Lord.
LAITY: Lord, have mercy.
PRIEST: For this Holy House and for those that enter it with faith, reverence and the fear of God, let us entreat the Lord.
LAITY: Lord, have mercy.
PRIEST: For our Archbishop . . . ., the local presbyters, the diaconate in Christ and for all the clergy and the people, let us entreat the Lord.
LAITY: Lord, have mercy.
PRIEST: For our God-fearing President . . . ., for all civil authorities, for all the American people and nation, let us beseech the Lord.
LAITY: Lord, have mercy.
PRIEST: For this city and for every city and land and for the faithful who dwell in them, let us beseech the Lord.

LAITY: Lord, have mercy.

PRIEST: For reasonable weather, for the abundance of the fruits of the earth and for peaceful times, let us beseech the Lord.

LAITY: Lord, have mercy.

PRIEST: For those that travel by land, by water, or by air, for the sick, for those that suffer, for captives and for their salvation, let us beseech the Lord.

LAITY: Lord, have mercy.

PRIEST: For our deliverance from all tribulation, wrath, danger and necessity, let us beseech the Lord.

LAITY: Lord, have mercy.

PRIEST: Help, save, comfort and protect us, O God, by Thy grace. Commemorating our most holy, pure, blessed and glorified Lady, Mother of God and Ever-Virgin Mary, with all the Saints, let us commend ourselves and one another and our whole life to Christ, our God.

LAITY: To Thee, O Lord.

PRIEST: For to Thee belong all glory, honor, and worship to the Father and to the Son and to the Holy Spirit, now and for ever and from all Ages to all Ages.

LAITY: Amen.

Part Two: The First Antiphon

This, the first of three Antiphons, was originally sung as a response to Psalm readings by the people. Later, two choirs sang them from either side of the Church. Some jurisdictions of the Orthodox Church still sing the 102 (103) Psalm in this place. Most, however, sing the Antiphons alone. You should participate by singing them with the choir, using their words as a private prayer, or meditating on the meaning of the hymn or the Psalm. You may also read the silent prayer said by the Priest.

LAITY: Amen. By the intercessions of the Mother of God, Savior, save us. (Three times)

PRIEST: (Inaudibly) O Lord, our God, Whose power is inconceivable and glory incomprehensible, Whose mercy is immeasurable and tenderness to man unspeakable, do Thou, O Master, according to Thy goodness, look down upon us and upon this Holy House and show us and those that pray with us the riches of Thy mercy and pity.

PRIEST: Again and again in peace let us bessech the Lord.

LAITY: Lord, have mercy.

PRIEST: Lord, have mercy.

PRIEST: Help, save, comfort and protect us, O God, with Thy favor. Commemorating our most holy, pure, blessed and glorified Lady, Mother of God and Ever-Virgin Mary, with all the Saints, let us commend ourselves and one another and our whole life, to Christ, our God.

LAITY: To Thee, O Lord.

PRIEST: For Thine is the might and Thine is the kingdom and th power and the glory of the Father and of the Son and of the Holy Spirit, now and for ever and from all Ages to all Ages.

LAITY: Amen.

Part Three: The Second Antiphon

As an Antiphon, this is repeated twice, though in some Orthodox jurisdictions 145 (146) Psalm is said instead of "Save us O Son of God . . ." It is followed by a beautiful hymn which is like a short creed, including reference to the two basic Christian beliefs— the Incarnation of Christ and the Holy Trinity. Sing along with the choir, use the words as private prayer, meditate on the meaning of the hymns, or read the prayer said by the Priest silently to yourself.

LAITY: O Son of God, Who didst rise from the dead, save us who sing to Thee: Alleluia. (Twice)

PRIEST: (Inaudibly) O Master, O Lord, our God, save Thy people and bless Thine inheritance; protect the whole body of Thy Church, and sanctify those who love the beauty of Thy House. Do Thou endow them with Thy divine Power and forsake not us who have set our hope in Thee.

LAITY: Glory to the Father and to the Son and to the Holy Spirit. Both now and ever and unto ages of ages. Amen.

PRIEST: (Inaudibly) O Thou Who hast given us grace at this time with one accord to make our common supplications unto Thee and dost promise, that when two

120

or three are gathered together in Thy Name, Thou wilt grant their requests; fulfill now, O Lord, the petitions of Thy servants, as may be the most expedient for them; granting us in this world knowledge of Thy Truth, and in the world to come life everlasting.

LAITY: O Only-begotten Son and Word of God, Who being Immortal, yet didst deign for our salvation to be incarnated through our most holy Lady and Ever-Virgin Mary, and without change didst become Man and wast crucified, by death overcoming death, do Thou, Christ our God, save us; Thou, Who are One of the Holy Trinity and art glorified with the Father and the Holy Spirit.

PRIEST: Again, yet again in peace let us entreat the Lord.

LAITY: Lord, have mercy.

PRIEST: Help, save, be merciful and protect us, O God, by Thy grace.

Commemorating our most holy, pure, blessed and glorified Lady, Mother of God and Ever-Virgin Mary, with all the Saints, let us commend ourselves and one another and our whole life to Christ our God.

LAITY: To Thee, O Lord.

PRIEST: For Thou, O God, art good and lovest mankind and to Thee we ascribe glory, to the Father and to the Son and to the Holy Spirit, now and ever and unto ages of ages.

LAITY: Amen.

Part Four: The Third Antiphon and the
"Little Entrance"

The choir now sings the third Antiphon which is one of the following eight "Dismissal Hymns of the Resurrection"—one each for the eight tones of Byzantine Music. In some jurisdictions the Beatitudes are sung at this time. However, in these jurisdictions the Dismissal Hymns are also sung after the "Little Entrance."

During the Great Lent, and following Easter other Hymns are sung each Sunday in accordance to the season. Read or sing or listen to the appropriate hymn for the day as the choir sings it.

Tone I

When the stone had been sealed by the Jews, and when the soldiers were watching Thy Sacred Body, Thou, O Savior, didst arise on the third day and give Life to the World. Wherefore the Powers of Heaven cried to Thee, O Giver of Life: Glory to Thy Resurrection, O Christ; glory to Thy kingdom; glory to Thy dispensation, O Thou Who alone art Merciful.

Tone II

When Thou, the Deathless Life, didst come down to Death, then didst Thou slay Hades through the dazzling brightness of the Godhead; and when Thou didst raise up from the Abyss, all the powers of the Heavens cried aloud; Christ our God, Giver of Life, glory to Thee.

Tone II

Let the Heavens rejoice, and let the Earth be glad, for the Lord hath shown strength with His arm: by death He hath trampled upon Death and become the First-Born of the dead; He hath delivered us from the depths of Hades, and to the world hath granted the Great Mercy.

Tone IV

The women disciples of the Lord learned from the Angel the joyous proclamation of the Resurrection, and the abolition of the ancestral sentence; and with pride they announced to the Apostles; Death is despoiled, Christ our God hath arisen, and giveth to the world the Great Mercy.

Tone Plagal I

Let us, the faithful, praise and worship the Word, co-eternal with the Father and the Spirit, and for our salvation born of a Virgin. For He will to be lifted up upon the Cross in the flesh, and to endure death, and to raise the dead by His glorious Resurrection.

Tone Plagal II

The Angelic Powers were before Thy tomb, the Watch became as dead, and Mary stood in the sepulchre and sought Thy Sacred Body. Thou despoiledst Hades, for Thou wast not tempted by it; Thou camest to the Virgin to give Life. O Lord, Who didst rise from the dead, glory to Thee.

Grave Tone

Thou hast destroyed Death by Thy Cross; Thou hast

opened Paradise to the thief; Thou hast changed the lamentation of the Myrrh-bearers into joy; and Thou hast commanded Thine Apostles to proclaim that Thou, O Christ our God, hast arisen and dost grant to the world the Great Mercy.

Tone Plagal IV

From on High, O Merciful Savior, Thou didst descend, and endure the grave for three days, that Thou mightest free us from anguish, Glory to Thee, O Lord, our Life and our Resurrection.

As the choir sings the Third Antiphon (one of the Dismissal Hymns for the Resurrection) the Priest reads the following prayer. Join him in this prayer said before the "Little Entrance."

PRIEST: (Inaudibly) O Master and Lord, our God, Who hast constituted the orders and armies of angels and archangels to do the service of Thy glory in Heaven, grant that there may be with our Entry, and Entry of Holy Angels, serving with us and with us glorifying Thee for Thy goodness. For to Thee belong all glory, honor, and worship, to the Father and to the Son and to the Holy Spirit now and for ever and from all Ages to Ages. Amen.

"The Little Entrance"

The Priest, preceded by the Altar Boys, comes out of the Altar area into the Nave bearing the Gospel Book. This procession is a symbol, representing one reason why Christ came into the world: to teach us God's truth and His will for us. What is your personal response to Christ the Teacher who now comes before you? We bow our heads in grateful reverence as the Priest chants the following words.

PRIEST: Wisdom! Let us arise!
LAITY: Come, let us worship and bow unto Christ. Save us, O Son of God, Who didst rise from the dead; save us who sing unto Thee: Alleluia.

After the Priest re-enters the Altar area and places the Gospel Book upon the Holy Table, the choir again sings the "Dismissal Hymn of the Resurrection" for a second time, thus making it an Antiphon (sung at least twice). This is followed by the singing of some additional hymns appropriate to the season, the Saint of the day, and the hymn of the Patron Saint of your parish Church. You can sing these hymns with the choir, pray their words as your own, or form a personal prayer based on their ideas.

PRIEST: Let us entreat the Lord.
LAITY: Lord, have mercy.
PRIEST: For Thou our God art holy, and to Thee we ascribe glory, to the Father and to the Son and to the Holy Spirit, now and ever, unto ages of ages.
LAITY: Amen.

Part Five: The Scripture Readings

The readings from the New Testament follow, showing concretely what the teaching of Christ is. We begin by singing the "Thrice-Holy Hymn" which is an act of adoration to God. Sing this hymn with the choir; or, repeat it once and read the prayer of the Priest with him; or, pray that God open up your heart to understand His teaching.

LAITY: Holy God, Holy and Mighty, Holy and Immortal have mercy upon us.
Glory to the Father and to the Son and to the Holy Spirit. Both now and ever and unto ages of ages. Amen.
Holy and Immortal, have mercy upon us.
Holy God, Holy and Mighty, Holy and Immortal, have mercy upon us.
PRIEST: (Inaudibly) O Holy God, Who restest among Thy Saints and art glorified by the Cherubim and praised by the Seraphim with Thrice-holy Voice, and worshipped by all the Host of Heaven; Thou Who hast brought all things out of nothingness into being; Thou Who hast created man in Thine Image and Likeness, and hast adorned him with all Thy favours; Thou Who givest to the suppliant wisdom add prudence and dost not neglect the sinner, but hast set forth the way of repentance unto salvation; Thou Who hast accounted us, Thy humble and unworthy servants, worthy to stand at this time before the glory of Thy Holy Altar and to bring to Thee meet adoration and praise; do Thou, Master, accept, even from

the mouth of us sinners, the Thrice-holy Hymn and visit us in Thy Righteousness; forgive us all our transgressions, voluntary and involuntary, sanctify our souls and bodies and grant that we may worship Thee in holiness all the days of our life; through the intercessions of Thy Holy Mother and all the Saints, who from the beginning of time have pleased Thee; for Thou, Our God, art holy and to Thee we ascribe glory, to the Father and to the Son and to the Holy Spirit, now and for ever and from all Ages to all Ages. Amen.

Reading of the Epistle

PRIEST: Wisdom!

READER: The reading (from the Acts of the Holy Apostles), (from the Epistle of the Holy Apostle. . . .) or (from the Epistle of Saint . . . .).

PRIEST: Let us attend.

READER: In those days (Brethren) or (My son) (continues with reading).

PRIEST: Peace unto thee, O Reader.

LAITY: Alleluia, alleluia, alleluia.

PRIEST: (Inaudibly) O Merciful Master, cause the pure light of the knowledge of Thee to shine in our hearts, and open the eyes of our mind to perceive Thy message of Good Tidings; fill us with the fear of Thy blessed commandment, that we, trampling down our fleshly desires, may seek a heavenly citizenship, and may do and consider all those things that are well pleasing to Thee. For Thou, Christ, our God, art the Source of Light to our souls and bodies, and to Thee we ascribe glory, with Thine Eternal Father and Thine all-holy, righteous, and life-giving Spirit, now and for ever and from all Ages to all Ages. Amen.

Reading of the Gospel

PRIEST: Wisdom! Attend! Let us hear the Holy Gospel. Peace unto all.

LAITY: And to thy spirit.

PRIEST: The reading from the Holy Gospel according to Saint . . . .

LAITY: Glory to Thee, O Lord, Glory to Thee.

PRIEST: Gives reading from the Holy Gospel.

LAITY: Glory to Thee, O Lord, glory to Thee.

(At this point some jurisdictions repeat some Litanies and pray on behalf of the dead and on behalf of the Catechumens. They conclude with "Help us, save us, have mercy on us, and keep us, O God by Thy Grace." All then say the concluding words of the shorter Litany and of this section:)

PRIEST: Grant that being ever protected by Thy power, to Thee we may ascribe glory, to the Father and to the Son and to the Holy Spirit, now ever and unto ages of ages.

LAITY: Amen.

Part Six: The Great Entrance—The Transfer of the Bread and Wine to the Holy Table

This part of the Divine Liturgy begins with the great "Cherubic Hymn." As the choir sings this Hymn in which we the worshippers are likened to the angels, the call is made to you to put away all worldly care and turn your mind fully to God and the acts of worship in the Divine Liturgy. Sing it with the choir; or read it prayerfully and read the prayer which the Priest says. As the Priest censes you, bow your head as a sign that you recognize that the incense symbolizes your prayer which rises heavenward and the gifts of God to us. Confess your sins at this time and ask God's pardon.

The Cherubic Hymn

LAITY: We who mystically represent the Cherubim, sing the Thrice-holy Hymn to the life-giving Trinity. Let us put away all worldly care, so that we may receive the King of All:

PRIEST: (Inaudibly) None is worthy, among them that are enslaved by carnal desires and pleasures to approach or come near or minister before Thee, the King of Glory; for Thy Service is great and fearful even to the Heavenly Powers. Yet since, through Thine ineffable and immeasurable compassion, Thou hast without change or differentation become man and taken the title of our High Priest, as Lord of All Thou has committed to us the celebration of this rite and of the Bloodless Sacrifice. For Thou, O Lord our God. alone dost govern all things in heaven and in earth, Thou Who sittest upon the throne of the Cherubim and art Lord of the Seraphim and King of Israel, Who only art Holy and restest among Thy Saints. To Thee I persistently call, for Thou alone art righteous and ready to hear. Look upon me Thy sinful and unprofitable servant and purify my soul and heart from an evil conscience; enable me by the power of Thy Holy Spirit, girt with the grace of the Priesthood to stand at this Thy Holy Table and to consecrate Thy Holy and Spotless Body and Thy Precious Blood. For to Thee I come near, bowing down my neck, and Thee I beseech. Turn not away Thy Face from me, neither reject me from among Thy children, but consider me worthy, so that these Gifts may be brought near to Thee by me, Thy sinful and unworthy servant. For Thou art the Offerer and the Offered, the Acceptor and the Distributed, Christ God, and to Thee we ascribe glory, with Thine Eternal Father and Thy most holy, righteous and life-giving Spirit, now and forever and from all Ages to all Ages. Amen.

"The Great Entrance"

The Priest, again preceded by the Altar Boys, now brings into the Sanctuary the Paten (on which is the Bread) and the Chalice (in which is the wine). On his back or shoulder, the Priest bears the "Aer Cloth" upon which is sewn a Cross. The "Great Entrance" is a symbolic act which points to another reason why Christ came into the world: to bear His Cross and die for our salvation. Christ is on His way to Golgotha for you! How do you respond? The Priest repeats the words of the pentitent thief who was crucified together with Christ; but he changes them to the plural to include you and all the members of the worshipping Church. Make these words your own. This is followed by the "Spiritual Litany."

> PRIEST: May the Lord, our God, remember us all in His Kingdom, now and ever, and unto ages of ages.
> LAITY: Amen.
> (The Priest enters the Sanctuary, places the Holy Gifts on the Holy Table and censes them. The choir concludes the Cherubic Hymn).
> LAITY: Invisibily attended by the Angelic Hosts, Alleluia.

"The Spiritual Litany"

Pray for the "things profitable unto our souls" as the Priest leads you in this Litany.

PRIEST: Let us complete our prayer to the Lord.

LAITY: Lord, have mercy.

PRIEST: For the Precious Gifts here presented, let us entreat the Lord.

LAITY: Lord, have mercy.

PRIEST: For our deliverance from all affliction, wrath, danger and neccessity, let us entreat the Lord.

LAITY: Lord, have mercy.

PRIEST: Help, save, be merciful and protect us, O God, by Thy grace.

PRIEST: For this whole day, that it may be perfect, holy, peaceful and sinless, let us entreat the Lord.

LAITY: Grant this, O Lord.

PRIEST: For an Angel of peace, a faithful Guide, a Guardian of our souls and bodies, let us entreat the Lord.

LAITY: Grant this, O Lord.

PRIEST: For His forgiveness and remission of our sins and transgression, let us entreat the Lord.

LAITY: Grant this, O Lord.

PRIEST: For things good and profitable unto our souls and for the peace of the world, let us entreat the Lord.

LAITY: Grant this, O Lord.

PRIEST: That we may complete the remainder of our lives in peace and penitence, let us entreat the Lord.

LAITY: Grant this, O Lord.

PRIEST: That the end of our lives may be Christian, without torment, blameless and peaceful, and for a good account at the fearsome judgement-seat of Christ, let us entreat the Lord.

LAITY: Grant this O Lord.

PRIEST: Commemorating our most holy, pure, blessed, and glorified Lady, Mother of God and Ever-Virgin Mary, with all the Saints, let us commend ourselves and one another and our whole life to Christ, our God.

LAITY: To Thee, O Lord.

PRIEST: Through the mercies of Thine Only-begotten Son, with Whom Thou are blessed, together with Thine All-Holy, good and life-giving Spirit, now and ever and unto ages of ages.

LAITY: Amen.

Part Seven: The Core of the Divine Liturgy; The Great Eucharistic Prayer

We have come to the core of the Divine Liturgy—its sacramental center, known as the "Great Eucharistic Prayer." Preceding it are a blessing, a hymn confessing our faith in the Holy Trinity, the Creed, the call to make the Offering, and the Apostolic blessing. There is much you can do to participate in this preliminary action preceding the "Great Eucharistic Prayer: sing the hymns, receive and return the blessings, recite the Creed.

PRIEST: Peace unto all.
LAITY: And with thy spirit.
PRIEST: Let us love one another, that we may with one mind confess:
LAITY: The Father, Son and Holy Spirit, Trinity, one in substance and undivided.
PRIEST: The doors, the doors; in wisdom let us attend.

The Creed

LAITY: I believe in one God, Father Almighty, Maker of Heaven and Earth and of everything visible and invisible.

And in one Lord Jesus Christ, the only-begotten Son of God, begotten of the Father before all Ages. Light of Light, True God of True God, begotten not made, co-substantial with the Father, through Whom all things were made.

Who for us men and for our salvation came down from Heaven, and was incarnated by the Holy Spirit and of the Virgin Mary, and became Man.

Crucified for our salvation under Pontius Pilate, He suffered and was buried.

And was resurrected on the third day according to the Scriptures.

And ascended into Heaven, and sat at the right hand of the Father;

And He will return in glory to judge the living and the dead; Whose Reign will have no end.

And I believe in the Holy Spirit, the Lord, the Giver of Life, Who proceeds from the Father, Who together with the Father and the Son, is worshipped and glorified; Who spoke through the Prophets.

I believe in One, Holy, Catholic and Apostolic Church.
I acknowledge One Baptism for the remission of sins.
I await for the resurrection of the dead. And the life
of the Ages to come.

LAITY: Amen.

PRIEST: Let us stand aright; let us stand in awe; let
us attend, that we may make the Holy Offering in peace.

LAITY: A mercy of peace; a sacrifice of praise.

PRIEST: The grace of our Lord Jesus Christ, and the
love of God the Father, and the communion of the Holy
Spirit be with you all.

LAITY: And with thy spirit.

PRIEST: Let us lift up our hearts.

LAITY: We lift them up unto the Lord.

PRIEST: Let us give thanks unto the Lord.

LAITY: It is meet and right.

"The Great Eucharistic Prayer"

This is the oldest part of the Divine Liturgy, its heart.
Here the most significant liturgical and sacramental activity takes place. It is one long prayer—some of it is
said aloud by the Priest; some of it is said inaudibly
by the Priest; some is sung by the choir. It is, however,
one long prayer. You are called to share in it word
by word.

"Remembrance"

The first thing which is done in the "Great Eucharistic
Prayer" is to "Remember" in a spirit of thankfulness
all that God has done for us, with special emphasis upon
the establishment and institution of the Sacrament of
the Holy Eucharist.

PRIEST: It is meet and right to hymn Thee, to bless Thee,
to praise Thee, to give thanks unto Thee, and to worship
Thee in every place of Thy dominion: for Thou art God
ineffable, inconceivable, invisible, incomprehensible, ever
existing, unchangeable. Out of nothing has Thou brought
us into being, and when we had fallen away, Thou didst
raise us up again and Thou hast not ceased to do all things
until You brought us back up to Heaven, and bestowed
upon us Thy kingdom which is to come. For all these

things, we give thanks unto Thee, and to Thine Only-Begotten Son, and to Thy Holy Spirit, for all the things of which we know, and for all the benefits both manifest and unseen, which have been bestowed upon us, and we give thanks unto Thee also for this ministry, which Thou dost vouchsafe to receive at our hands, even though there stand beside Thee thousands of Archangels and ten thousands of Angels, the Cherubim and the Seraphim, six-winged, many-eyed, soaring aloft, borne on their wings, (aloud) Singing, voicing, proclaiming and saying the triumphal hymn:

LAITY: Holy, holy, holy, Lord of Hosts, heaven and earth are full of Thy Glory. Hosanna in the Highest; blessed is He that cometh in the Name of the Lord. Hosanna in the Highest.

PRIEST: (Inaudibly) With these blessed Powers we also, O Master Who lovest mankind, cry out and say: Holy art Thou, and all Holy, Thou, and Thine Only-Begotten Son, and Thy Holy Spirit; Holy art Thou and all Holy, and majestic is Thy glory; Who so loved the world as to give Thine Only-Begotten Son, that everyone who believeth in Him shouldst not perish, but have everlasting life; And He, when He had come, fulfilling all the dispensation appointed for us, on the night in which He was betrayed, or together, in which He gave up Himself for the life of the world, took bread in His holy, pure, and blameless hands; and when He had given thanks, and had blessed, hallowed, and broken it, He gave it to His Holy Disciples and Apostles, saying:

PRIEST: Take ye, eat: This is My Body, Which for you is broken, unto remission of sins.

LAITY: Amen.

PRIEST: (Inaudibly) Likewise after Supper the Cup, saying:

PRIEST: Drink ye all of this: This is my Blood of the New Testament, which is shed for you and for many, for the remission of sins.

LAITY: Amen.

PRIEST: (Inaudibly) Bearing in remembrance therefore, the commandment of Salvation, the Cross, the Grave, the Resurrection on the third day, the Ascension into heavin, the sitting at the Right Hand and the Second and glorious Coming.

"Offering"

The next element of the "Great Eucharistic Prayer" is the Offering of the Bread and the Wine to God, which the Laity do through the Priest with the following words as he lifts up the Chalice and Paten toward God.

PRIEST: Thy Gifts, of what is Thine, do we offer to Thee, in all we do and for all Thy blessings.

"Consecration"

The Priest calls upon God to consecrate the Bread and Wine and make them Body and Blood of Christ. We are present before the crucified Lord who has given Himself for the salvation of the whole world, including ourselves. With what gratitude and humility do we receive this blessing? The Choir softly sings our praises as the Priest prays for the consecration. Join the choir singing; prayerfully share the prayers of consecration with the Priest; contemplate the Crucified Lord at this most holy moment. During this moment, which is the loftiest and most sacred in the Divine Liturgy, the choir sings the following hymn in soft and reverent tones.

LAITY: We praise Thee, we bless Thee, we give thanks unto Thee, O Lord, and we entreat Thee, O our God.
(The Priest prays inaudibly and invokes the Holy Spirit to come upon the Precious Gifts).
PRIEST: (Inaudibly) Again we offer to Thee this reasonable and bloodless Service, and we ask and pray and supplicate: send down Thy Holy Spirit upon us and upon these Gifts here presented.
(The Priest blesses the Bread on the Paten).
And make this Bread the Precious Body of Thy Christ. Amen.
(Then he blesses the Wine in the Chalice)
And that which is in this Cup, the Precious Blood of Thy Christ. Amen.
(Finally, he blesses both Paten and Chalice with the following words).
Changing (Them) by Thy Holy Spirit. Amen, Amen, Amen.

"Commemoration"

The "Great Eucharistic Prayer" now comes to its

conclusion with the "Commemoration" in which we note for whom this sacrifice has been offered. A careful reading of the hymns and prayers will lead you to the conclusion that we have offered this Sacrament to God on behalf of everyone in the whole world.

So that They may be to those that receive Them for the purification of the soul, for the remission of sins, for the fellowship of Thy Holy Spirit, for the fulfillment of Thy Holy Spirit, for the fulfillment of the Kingdom of Heaven, and for the boldness to approach Thee, neither unto judgment nor unto condemnation. Again we offer unto Thee this reasonable Service for those who have fallen asleep in the Faith, Forefathers, Fathers, Patriarchs, Prophets, Apostles, Preachers, Evangelists, Martyrs, Confessors, Ascetics, and every righteous spirit in faith made perfect.

PRIEST: Especially for our most holy, pure, blessed, glorified Lady, Mother of God and Ever-Virgin, Mary.

LAITY: It is very meet to bless Thee, Theotokos, the ever-blessed and most pure Virgin and Mother of our God. Thee that art more honorable than the Cherubim and incomparably more glorious than the Seraphim, that, without spot of sin, didst bear God, the Word; Thee, verily the Birth-giver of God, do we magnify.

(On the great festivals, instead of the above, other hymns are sung).

PRIEST: (Inaudibly) For holy John the Baptist, Prophet and Forerunner, for the holy, glorious, and honorable Apostles, for Saint (of the day) whose memory we celebrate, and for all Thy Saints, by whose supplication do Thou, O God, visit us. Be mindful also of those who slumber in the hope of a resurrection to everlasting life. (He commemorates whom he will.) Give them rest, O God, where the light of Thy countenance shineth. Further, we entreat Thee, O Lord, be mindful of every Bishopric of the Orthodox, that they may teach Thy Truth aright, of all ecclesiastical rules, of the diaconate in Christ, and of all clerical and monastic orders. Further, we offer to Thee this reasonable service for the World, for the Holy, Catholic and Apostolic Church, for those living in purity and temperance, for our most faithful and Christian Kings, and for their whole court and army. Give to them, O Lord, peace in their kingdoms, that we also may have tranquillity in their calm, and may pass a peaceful life in all piety and temperance;

PRIEST: Above all, be mindful, O Lord, of our Archbishop . . . , guard him for Thy Holy Churches in peace, with safety, honor, health, and length of days, to teach aright the Word of Thy Truth.

PRIEST: (Inaudibly) Be mindful O Lord, of the city in which we sojourn and of every city and land of the faithful who dwell in them. Be mindful, O Lord, of those that travel by land, by water, or by air, of the sick, of those that suffer, of captives and of their salvation. Be mindful, O Lord, of those that serve and bring forth fruit in Thy Holy Churches and of those who remember the poor, and upon all of us send down Thy Mercies.

PRIEST: And grant to us with one mouth and one heart to glorify and praise Thine all honorable and Majestic Name, of the Father, and of the Son and of the Holy Spirit; now and ever, and unto ages of ages.

LAITY: Amen.

The closing portion of this section whose highlight is the "Great Eucharistic Prayer" consists of the Spiritual Litany, the Lord's Prayer, a blessing and a final prayer of Thanksgiving. Participate by praying the Litany, sharing in the blessing and the prayers. The Priest blesses:

PRIEST: And the mercies of the Great God and our Savior Jesus Christ shall be with you all.

LAITY: And with thy spirit.

PRIEST: Having commemorated all the Saints, again and again in peace let us entreat the Lord.

LAITY: Lord, have mercy.

PRIEST: For these Precious Gifts, which have been offered and sanctified, let us entreat the Lord.

LAITY: Lord, have mercy.

PRIEST: That our merciful God, Who hath received Them at His holy and celestial and invisible Altar, unto a breath of spiritual fragrance, send down upon us divine grace and the gift of the Holy Spirit.

LAITY: Lord, have mercy.

PRIEST: For our deliverance from all tribulations, wrath, danger and necessity, let us beseech the Lord.

LAITY: Lord, have mercy.

PRIEST: (Inaudibly) To Thee, O Merciful Master, we

confide our whole life and hope, and Thee we ask and pray and supplicate. Deem us worthy to receive Thy Heavenly and Awful Mysteries of this holy and spiritual Table with a pure conscience, for the remission of sins, for the pardon of transgressions, for the fellowship of the Holy Spirit, for the inheritance of the Kingdom of Heaven, for boldness to approach Thee, neither unto judgment nor unto condemnation.

PRIEST: Help, save, comfort and protect us. O God, by thy Grace. For this whole day, that it may be perfect, holy, peaceful and sinless, let us entreat the Lord.

LAITY: Grant this, O Lord.

PRIEST: For an angel of Peace, a faithful guide, guardian of our souls and bodies, let us entreat the Lord.

LAITY: Grant this, O Lord.

PRIEST: For forgiveness and remission of our sins and transgressions, let us entreat the Lord.

LAITY: Grant this, O Lord.

PRIEST: For those things that are good and profitable for our souls and for the peace of the world, let us entreat the Lord.

LAITY: Grant this, O Lord.

PRIEST: That the remainder of our lives may be passed in peace and penitence, let us entreat the Lord.

LAITY: Grant this, O Lord.

PRIEST: That the end of our lives may be Christian, without torment, blameless and peaceful, and that we may have a good defence before the fearful Judgment Seat of Christ, let us entreat the Lord.

LAITY: Grant this, O Lord.

PRIEST: Asking for the unity of the Faith and for the communion of the Holy Spirit, let us commend ourselves and one another and our whole life to Christ our God.

LAITY: To Thee, O Lord.

PRIEST: And render us, O Master, worthy, that we may boldly without condemnation dare to call upon Thee the Heavenly God, as Father, and to say:

The Lord's Prayer

LAITY: Our Father, Who art in heaven, hallowed be Thy name; Thy kingdom come; Thy will be done on earth as it is in heaven. Give us this day our daily bread. And forgive us our trespasses as we forgive those who trespass against us. And lead us not into temptation; but deliver us from evil.

PRIEST: For Thine is the Kingdom and the power and the glory, of the Father and of the Son and of the Holy Spirit, now and ever and unto ages of ages.

LAITY: Amen.

PRIEST: Peace unto all.

LAITY: And with thy spirit.

PRIEST: Let us bow our heads unto the Lord.

LAITY: To Thee, O Lord.

PRIEST: (Inaudibly) We give thanks to Thee, O King Invisible, Who by Thy boundless power hast formed all things, and by the fullness of Thy Mercy hast brought forth all things out of nothingness into being. Do Thou Thyself, O Master, look down from Heaven upon those who have bowed down their heads before Thee; for they have bowed not before flesh and blood, but before Thee, Almighty God. Do Thou, therefore, O Master, administer these Offerings to all of us for good, according to the special need of each of us; do Thou travel with those that travel, by land, by water, or by air; and do Thou, Physician of our souls and bodies, heal those of us who are sick,

PRIEST: Through the grace and mercy and love for men of Thine only-begotten Son, with Whom Thou art blessed, with Thine all-holy, and good and life-giving Spirit, now and ever and unto ages of ages.

LAITY: Amen.

Part Eight: The Holy Communion

The choir sings the Communion Anthem "Praise ye the Lord from the Heavens" as the Priest prepares the consecrated elements for Holy Communion. He receives Holy Communion first, then he comes forth with the Chalice offering the Body and Blood of Our Lord—the source of new life and union with God—to the faithful. If you are to receive Holy Communion, repeat the prayers which the Priest says before Holy Communion. If you are not going to receive, pray for those who do and join in the hymns. Plan to receive Holy Communion as often as possible. Frequent Holy Communion is the best way to participate in the Divine Liturgy.

PRIEST: (Inaudibly) Hearken, O Lord Jesus Christ our God, from Thy Holy dwelling-place and from the Throne of glory of Thy Kingdom, and come and sanctify us, Thou Who sittest above with the Father and art here invisibly present with us, and do Thou deign by Thy mighty power to give to us of Thy Sacred Body and of Thy Precious Blood, and through us to all the people.

PRIEST: Let us attend. Holy things unto the holy.

LAITY: One is Holy, One is Lord, Jesus Christ, to the glory of God the Father. Amen.

The Communion Anthem

LAITY: Praise ye the Lord from the Heavens. Alleluia. (Three times)

(On the great Festivals the Communion Hymn of the Festival is sung. The Priest breaks the now Consecrated Bread into four portions).

PRIEST: (Inaudibly) The Lamb of God is broken and distributed; broken but not sundered, always fed upon and never consumed but sanctifying those who partake.

(He places one portion in the Chalice as he says these words:)

The fullness of the Cup, of Faith, and of the Holy Spirit. Amen.

(The following words are said as he blesses a vessel of boiling water brought by an Altar boy):

Blessed is the ardor of Thy Saints, now and for ever and from all Ages to all Ages.

(The Priest pours the hot water into the Chalice as he says):

The ardor of Faith, of the fullness of the Holy Spirit. Amen.

(The Priest repeats the "Prayers before Holy Communion." Join in these prayers if you are going to receive Holy Communion.)

I believe, O Lord, and confess that Thou art verily the Christ, the Son of the Living God, Who didst come into the World to save sinners, of whom I am the chief. Also I believe that This is Thy Sacred Body and This Thy Precious Blood. Therefore I pray Thee, have mercy upon me and pardon my transgressions, voluntary and involuntary, in word and in deed, both known and unknown, and consider me worthy, without condemnation, to participate in Thy Sacred Mysteries, unto the remission of sins and unto Life Everlasting. Amen.

Receive me today, O Son of God, as a partaker of Thy Mystic Feast; for I will not speak of the Mystery to Thine enemies; I will confess Thee: Lord, remember me when Thou comest in Thy Kingdom.

May the Communion of Thy holy mysteries be neither to my judgment nor to my condemnation, O Lord, but to the healing of both soul and body.

Behold, I draw near to Christ, our Immortal King and God.

(The Priest first receives the Body of our Lord):

To me (name), the Priest, is given the most Holy and Precious Body of our Lord God and Savior Jesus Christ, unto the remission of my sins and unto Eternal Life.

(Then he drinks from the Chalice):

The most Holy and Precious Blood of our Lord God and Savior Jesus Christ is given to me (name), the Priest, unto the remission of my sins and unto Eternal Life.

(After Communing, he kisses the Chalice and then places the particles of the Consecrated Bread into the Chalice):

This hath touched my lips, and my iniquity shall be taken away and my sin covered.

(He thanks God for the blessing of Holy Communion)

We thank Thee, O Merciful Master and Lover of our souls, that Thou hast this day vouchsafed to give us Thy Heavenly and Immortal Mysteries; direct us into the right way, strengthen all of us in Thy fear, watch over our life, make our footsteps safe, through the prayers and supplications of the glorious Mother of God and Ever-Virgin Mary and of all Thy Saints.

(At the end of the Communion Anthem he comes forth holding the Chalice and says):

PRIEST: With fear of God, with faith and with love, draw near.

(If you are prepared to partake of the Holy Communion, draw near at this time and receive. As you approach the Chalice, say the prayer which follows):

"Remember me, O Lord, when Thou comest in Thy Kingdom."

(After Communion thank God for the great gift of which He has rendered you worthy. Read the prayer of Thanksgiving as follows:)

Glory to Thee, O God! (Three times) "O Lord Jesus Christ, my God and Savior, I thank Thee for all Thy precious, immortal and life-giving Mysteries. I entreat Thee, O Lord of Mercy, grant me Thy protection, and keep me clean in heart and mind until the end of my life, that I may receive Thy Body and Blood as Thy worthy servant. For Thou art the Bread of Life and the source of Sanctification and the Giver of all good things. I bless Thy Holy Name, of the Father, of the Son, and of the Holy Spirit, now and ever. Amen.

"By the intercession of all Thy Saints and of Thy Holy Mother, grant us Thy peace, O Lord, and be gracious unto us. Amen."

(The Priest raises the Chalice high and blesses the people, saying the following words):

PRIEST: O God, save Thy people and bless Thine heritage.

LAITY: We have seen the pure Light, we have received the Heavenly Spirit, we have found the true Faith, worshipping the Undivided Trinity, Who hath saved us.

(On the great Festivals the Dismissal Hymn of the Festival is sung, instead of the above. Censing the Holy Gifts the Priest prays the following prayer, reminiscent of the Ascension of our Lord):

PRIEST: (Inaudibly) Be Thou exalted, O God, above the Heavens and Thy Glory above all the earth (three times). Blessed is our God.

PRIEST: Always, now and ever and unto ages of ages.

LAITY: Amen.

PRIEST: Let us arise. Having duly received the divine, holy, pure, immortal, heavenly, life-giving and awesome Mysteries of Christ, worthily let us give thanks unto the Lord.

Help, save, have mercy and protect us, O Lord, by Thy grace.

Entreating the Lord that this whole day may be perfect, holy, peaceful and sinless, let us commend ourselves and one another and our whole life to Christ, our God.

LAITY: To Thee, O Lord.

PRIEST: For Thou art our sanctification and to Thee we ascribe the glory, to the Father and the Son and to the Holy Spirit, now and for ever and unto ages of ages.

LAITY: Amen.

Part Nine: The Dismissal

The Divine Liturgy now comes to an end. Join the Priest in praying the prayer before the Icon of the Lord and sing the joyous hymn, "Blessed be the name of the Lord . . ." and join in the concluding prayers.

PRIEST: Let us go forth in peace, praying to the Lord.

LAITY: Lord, have mercy.

PRIEST: O Lord, Who blessest those who bless Thee and sanctifiest those who put their trust in Thee, save Thy people and bless Thine heritage; protect the whole body of Thy Church, and sanctify those who love the beauty of Thy House. Do Thou glorify them by Thy divine power and forsake not us who set our hope in Thee. Grant peace to Thy world, to Thy Churches, to the Priesthood, to our Rulers, to the armed forces and to all Thy people. For all good giving and every perfect gift is from above, coming down from Thee, the Father of light; and to Thee we ascribe glory and thanksgiving and worship, to the Father and to the Son and to the Holy Spirit, now and ever and unto ages of ages.

LAITY: Amen. Blessed be the Name of the Lord, from this time forth and forever more. (Three times)

PRIEST: (Inaudibly) O Christ, our God, Who art Thyself the Fulfillment of the Law and the Prophets, and hast fulfilled all the dispensation of the Father, do Thou always fill our hearts with joy and gladness, now and forever and from all Ages to all Ages. Amen.

PRIEST: Let us entreat the Lord.

LAITY: Lord, have mercy. (Three times) Holy father, give the blessing.

PRIEST: May the blessing of the Lord and His mercy come upon you through His divine grace and love for mankind; always, now and ever and unto ages of ages.

Glory to Thee, O God our hope, glory to Thee.

May Christ, our true God, Who rose from the dead, have mercy upon us, through the intercession of His most pure and Holy Mother; through the power of the precious and life-giving Cross; the protection of the sublime Spiritual Powers in Heaven; the supplications of the precious, glorious Prophet and Forerunner John the Baptist; of the holy, glorious and victorious Martyrs; of our saintly and God-inspired Fathers; of the holy and righteous ancestors Joachim and Anna; of Saint (of the day), whose memory

140

we celebrate, and of all the Saints, and may Christ save us, for He is gracious and loveth mankind.

LAITY: Protect, O Lord, unto many years him who blesseth us and bringeth us Thy Grace.

PRIEST: Through the prayers of our holy Fathers have mercy upon us, O Lord Jesus Christ, our God.

LAITY: Amen.

NOTES

6   The article first appeared in a parish bulletin and was subsequently republished in many places. For example, "Kimisis Theotokou," Easter, 1969, Volume XXVIII, No. 173.

7   For my view on the language question, please see my article "An Orthodox Answer to the Language Question: Flexible Bilingualism" in "The Orthodox Observer" November, 1970, year XXXVI, No. 608, p. 9.

13   The reference to God's perfection, and ours, comes from Jesus' Sermon on the Mount found in Matthew 5:48.

Not only does the creation story refer to man's creation in God's Image and Likeness (Genesis 1:26 and 27 and 9:6), but so does the New Testament (1 Corinthians 11:7; 2 Corinthians 3:18; Colossians 3:10). In Romans 8:29 we are told that we are destined by God "to be conformed to the image of His Son."

14   The story of Adam and Eve is told in three chapters in the book of Genesis—Chapter 1:26-29 and Chapter 2:7-8, 17-25 and Chapter 3:1-34.

15   St. Athanasios. "The Word became flesh, so as to make man receptive to the divine . . . for God became man so that we could become gods . . . He was incarnated so that He could make us divine in Him . . . and we consequently become a holy race, and communicants of divine grace." *On the Incarnation of the Word 54. Against Arians* 1:38, 39 and II:47, 70. *To Adelphion 4.*

Of course, St. John of Damascus clarifies this terminology by noting that man "is made divine by sharing in the divine light and not by transformation into divine essence." *Exposition of the Orthodox Faith* 11, 12.

This concept of growth is emphasized in Ephesians 4:15, 2 Peter 2:9 and Romans 8:29 as well as elsewhere in the Scriptures.

16 Archim. Christopher G. Stavropoulos, *Communicants of Divine Nature* (Greek) (Athens: 1972), p. 67.

19 Romans 8:26.

20 1 Peter 2:9. *The Orthodox Liturgical and Mystagogical Sermon* (Greek) Evangelos D. Theodorou (Athens, 1960) pp. 13, 15.

21 The modern Greek Edition of *The Life In Christ* was published under the title "E Christianike Zoe" (Athens: "Zoe" Publications, 1954) pp. 17-18.

22 Gospel passages referring to the institution of the Eucharist are Matthew 26:26-28; Mark 14:22-24; Luke 22:19-20.
    The intent of the Lord to be understood literally regarding His Body and Blood is recorded in John 6:52-56.

23 Panagiotes Trembelas, *Dogmatics of the Orthodox Catholic Church Ekklesias* (Greek) Athens: "O Soter" Publications, 1961). Volume 3, especially pages 216-238.
    St. John of Damascus, *Exposition of the Orthodox Faith*, Book IV, Chapter XIII.

24 The idea that the Divine Liturgy is the Church's self-expression is emphasized by Alexander Schmemann, *Introduction to Liturgical Theology*, Tr. by Asheleigh E. Moorehouse. (Portland, Maine: The American Orthodox Press, 1966), p. 165.
    The Eucharist as a healing and victorious power over sin and death is taught by St. Ignatios, *Epistle to the Ephesians*. XX.
    Theodoritos. *Commentary on Hebrews* 8:4.

25 St. Paul's description is the earliest of the New Testament accounts of the Last Supper. 2 Corinthians 11:23-26.

25- 26 Panagiotes Trembelas, *Ibid.*, Volume 3, p. 142.

28 This comment about the length and relevancy of the Divine Liturgy was made to me by a Church Council member early in my Priesthood. It helped motivate me to write this book.

32 The earliest description of the Eucharist is found in 1 Corinthians 11:23ff.

39 Timothy Ware, *The Orthodox Church* (Baltimore: Penguin Books, 1964), pp. 286-288.

41 R. M. French, *The Eastern Orthodox Church* (London: Hutchinson University Library, 1951).

42 *Ibid.*, p. 124.

47 1 Timothy 3:15
    Ephesians 1:23
    Colossians 1:24
    St. Basil, 11th Homily on Ephesians 1; 62, 81.

48 St. Basil, 4th Homily on Ephesians, 4.
    St. John Chrysostom, Homily on 2nd Corinthians, 3, 7.
    1 Peter 2:5, 2:9.

49 Peter Mogila, *Orthodox Confession of Faith of the Catholic and*

Apostolic Faith of the East, Question 108 in J. Karmiris, *The Dogmatic and Symbolic Monuments of The Eastern Orthodox Church* (Greek) (Athens: 1953), Volume II, page 640.

51   Gerasimos Papadopoulos, *Greek Philosophy As Preparation for Christianity* (Greek) (Athens: 1954), p. 22.
    Constitutions of the Holy Apostles Book VIII, Sec. II, vi. *Ibid.*, Book II, Section VII.

52   St. Cyprian, *Epistle* LIII, 2, 4, 5.

53   Alexander Schmemann, *op. cit.*, p. 166.

54   St. Maximos the Confessor, *Concerning Theology* 3rd century, St. Isaias the Anchorite, *Concerning the Attentive Mind* (Greek), *Philokalia Ton Ieron Niptikon* (Athens: Aster Publications, 1957), Volume 1, p. 32, section 13. Nicholas Cabasilas, *A Commentary on the Divine Liturgy.* Tr. by J. M. Hussey & P. A. McNulty. (London: (S.P.C.K., 1966), p. 34.

54- 55 St. Cyprian, *Epistle* LXXV, 5.

56   Oswald Spengler, *The Decline of the West: Form and Actuality.* (New York: Alfred A. Knopf, 1950), pp. 176-177 . . . "While the Gothic style soars, the Ionic hovers. The interior of the cathedral pulls up with primeval force, but the temple is laid down in majestic rest."

58   Joseph Ryksert, *Church Building* (New York: Hawthorn Books, 1966), pp. 10-11.

58- 59 Meletius Michael Solovey, *The Byzentine Divine Liturgy: History and Commentary.* Translated by Demetrios Emil Wysochansky. (Washington: Catholic University of America Press, 1970), p. 238 and p. 96.

62   Matthew 26:30; Mark 14:26. *Constitutions of the Holy Apostles* Book II, Section VII, LXXX.

64   1 Corinthians 14:15-16.
    For the original form of the Creed, see Ioannis Karmiris, *op. cit.*, Volume 1, p. 60. Luke 11:1-4 and Matthew 6:9-13.

65   Isaiah 29:13.

67   Galatians 6:14

68   *Constitutions of the Holy Apostles* Book II, Section VII, LIX.

71   Book II, Section VII, LXI.
    St. Isaac The Syrian, *Directions on Spiritual Training* in *Early Fathers from the Philokalia.* Tr. By E. Kadlovbousky and G. E. Palmer (London: Faber & Faber, 1954), p. 197, sec. 54.

72   Nicholas Cabasilas, *op. cit.*, p. 52.

74   Romans 8:26.
    Nicholas Cabasilas, *op. cit.*, p. 45.

75   Demetrios Panagiotopoulos *Interpretation of the Divine Liturgy* (Greek) (Athens: Zoe Brotherhood, 1927), p. 49.

78   Nicholas Cabasilas, *op. cit.*, p. 50.

79   *Constitutions of the Holy Apostles*, Book II, Section VII, LVII. See also J. H. Swraley, *The Early History of the Liturgy* 2nd Edition. (Cambridge: University Press, 1949). pp. 45, 122. The

Greek is "ho laos ta akrostiha hypopsalleto."

Nicholas Cabasilas, *op. cit.*, p. 51.

Nikolai Gogol *Meditations on the Divine Liturgy* (Jordonville, N. Y.: Holy Trinity Monastery Press, 1952), p. 19.

82   Demetrios Panagiotopoulos, *op. cit.*, pp. 86, 88.

83   Nikolai Gogol, *op. cit.*, p. 22.

86   2 Timothy 3:16-17.

90   Hebrews 2:19.

91   "Jesus, remember me when you come into your Kingdom" Luke 23:42.

92   Theodore of Mopsuestia quoted in Dom Gregory Dix, *The Shape of the Liturgy* (Westminster, England: Dacre Press, 1945), p. 282.

Nicholas Cabasilas, *op. cit.*, page 64.

Symeon, Archbishop of Thessalonike, "Concerning the Holy Service of the Divine Liturgy" in *Ta Apanta* (Greek) (Thessalonike: Regopoulos Publishers, n.d., p. 125.

93   Regarding the histories of the Entrances see Panagiotes Trempelas, *The Three Liturgies* (Greek) (Athens: The Patriarchal Scholarly Committee for the Revision and Publication of the Liturgical Books, 1935) pp. 37-38 and 82. See also, *The Religious and Ethical Encyclopedia* (Greek) Volume 8, p. 187.

96   Sophocles, *The Liturgy of the Orthodox Church* (Athens: Damascus Press, 1955) p. 100.

99   Nikolai Gogol, *op. cit.*, p. 36.

99-100 Demetrios Panagiotopoulos, *op. cit.*, pp. 175-176.

Constitutions of the Holy Apostles Book II, Section VII, LVII.

100   Swraley explains: "Hebrews XIII 15. The phrase *Thusian aineseos*, (Sacrifice of praise) in the LXX is a translation of the Hebrew (words) which denotes the highest form of the peace offering, the thank offering. See Lev. VII, 12." *op. cit.*, p. 16, note 6.

2 Corinthians 13:14.

101   The commandment of the Lord to conduct the Eucharist in His memory is found in Luke 22:19 and 1 Corinthians 11:24.

103   Isaiah 6:3.

105   The description of Christ's agony in Gethsemane when He offered Himself for us is found in Matthew 26:36-46 and Mark 14:32-42.

Nicholas Cabasilas, *op. cit.*, p. 70.

106   2 Corinthians 5:15.

107   See 2 Corinthians 1:3 for a passage which parallels this liturgical blessing.

109   Nicholas Cabasilas, *op. cit.*, p. 87.

Ibid., p. 88

110   Matthew 7:6 "Do not give to the dogs what is holy; and do not throw your pearls before swine."

112   Revelation 1:5-6.

Galatians 2:20.